KNOWING
DaNCE

"I know noth-
ing, except what
everyone knows
– if there when
Grace dances,
I should dance."

W.H. Auden

KNOWING DANCE

A Guide for Creative Teaching

Marion Gough

DANCE BOOKS
Cecil Court London

Published in 1999 by
Dance Books Ltd
15 Cecil Court
London WC2N 4EZ

www.dancebooks.co.uk

ISBN 1 85273 070 6

A CIP catalogue record for this book
is available from the British Library

Contents

Introduction   7

1 Teaching and Learning   1

Teachers and 'Philosophies'   1

The Student as Learner   4

Towards a Philosophy of Teaching and Learning   5

Defining Good Practice   6

'Good' and 'Bad' Teaching   10

Engaging Students in the Activity   11

Beginning with Ourselves   13

Learning Styles   14

Motivation   16

Equal Opportunities   18

2 Planning a Dance Course   23

Knowing Your Students   23

Aims and Objectives   25

Course Content   26

The Structure of a Creative Dance Class   26

Structure of a Lesson – An Example   32

Teaching Methods   34

Example of a Lesson Plan Using Different Styles and Strategies   38

Criteria for the Unexpected   40

Corrections   42

Repetition 43

Making Dance Expressive 45

First Encounters 46

Starting Class 50

Endings 51

Assessment and Evaluation 52

3 Composing, Performing, Appreciating 59

Composing 63

Performing 73

Appreciating 91

4 Promoting Good Practice 99

Teaching Skills for Dancers 99

A Training Programme 104

Evaluation 107

Enhancing Practice 116

Acknowledgements

I am particularly grateful to Alysoun Tomkins, Madalena Victorino, David Steele, Maggie Semple, Erica Stanton, Amanda Gough, Jane Mooney – all exceptional dance educators – for their inspiration, advice and support; to Raymond Johnston for his continued encouragement; and to those colleagues who have generously contributed to this book. Thanks to Bob for his patience and advice during the whole process.

This book is dedicated to Bill – a good friend and a wonderful dancer.

Introduction

An important feature of the arts is that they allow us to play.

> It is in playing and only in playing that the individual child or adult is able to be creative and to use the whole personality, and it is only in being creative that the individual discovers the self.
>
> D. W. Winnicott, *Playing and Reality* (Routledge, 1982)

Adults can become bogged down with responsibility at work and at home. Children increasingly spend time on their own in front of television or computers. We hear reports of primary school children being less fit than those of previous generations. It would appear to be particularly important that, in an increasingly stressful world, children and adults are given opportunities to play and to be creative.

The arts provide an environment for this to happen. They have much in common, and can support and stimulate each other, but they are not interchangeable.

> Each art form has its own distinctive features, history, body of knowledge, discipline, and artistic products. Each also has inherent artistic experience that is different from and complementary to other art disciplines.
>
> National Curriculum Council, HMSO, 1991

The art forms *are* different. They each offer their own ways of expressing what we think and feel about ourselves and the world around us. It in interesting, then, to consider why we chose to pursue a particular art form. What are its unique and special qualities? Why dance?

We may have chosen dance because it may be the primary, most immediate, form of expression for us. The expressive and social nature of dance gives us legitimate ways in which to invent, explore, solve problems – and have fun!

As teachers, how can we ensure that our students get the most out of dance? How can we match the illogicality of art with the logicality of method? Are we flexible enough to provide our students with opportunities which encourage thoughtful feeling and applaud spontaneity?

In his lecture 'The Agony and the Ecstasy' (Barbican Centre, London, 1997), John Tusa spoke about art as exploring confusion and defining disorder. To an inexperienced teacher, this uncertainty and unpredictability can appear frightening – not having all the answers, not being sure what to do next. Good teaching, however, requires us to be curious. Teachers should be concerned with developing their knowledge and skills. We need to find ways to keep our work fresh and alive; not to become too comfortable with the familiar but to consider new material and new methods – not only to keep our students actively involved but also so that we ourselves remain interested and challenged. We need to think of ourselves as learners on a journey towards personal growth in which questions are more important than answers – a journey that has no point of arrival but is a continuous exploration for learning.

This book aims to appeal to dancers who are new to teaching, as well as to experienced practitioners, by addressing questions not only about current concerns but also the universal issues which face all teachers of dance. It is intended for educators and dancers – and, of course, those involved in both fields. It does assume some knowledge of these areas, and goes more deeply into some areas explored in *In Touch With Dance* (Gough, 1996), namely:

- How to plan, deliver, assess and evaluate dance
- The three strands of the 'dance as art' model – composing, performing, appreciating

In addition, it considers philosophies of teaching and learning in an attempt to define and achieve good practice.

Contributions are included from a number of eminent practitioners in the field of dance, and the book should have relevance for community dance workers, teachers in schools, teachers in training, education units of dance companies, and dancers who are considering teaching.

If we consider education as an enabling process, giving access to power through knowledge and skills, then teaching is a political act. For me, most importantly it is about influencing change – change in attitudes to dance, and to the teaching of dance.

1

Teaching and Learning

Teachers and 'Philosophies'

What a teacher does – at any level, and in any context – is fashioned by a *set of philosophies*. These 'philosophies' may be implicit rather than explicit: we may not articulate them in this kind of way (although perhaps we should be able to do so). The way in which a teacher organises a dance class, for example, will tend to reflect her/his views of:

- The nature of knowledge – in particular the nature of dance knowledge.
- The nature of teaching and learning.
- Human nature – that is, of the child or student.

The nature of knowledge:

- Is 'knowledge' something which exists 'out there' in some objective, unchanging form?
- Or is knowledge a social product, created as a result of interaction between people (such as teachers and students) and their environment? Is this knowledge more like an 'integration' than a 'collection'?

  Basil Bernstein, 'On the Classification and Framing of Educational Knowledge', in R. Brown (ed.) *Knowledge, Education and Cultural Change*, (Tavistock, 1973).

The nature of teaching and learning:

- Is the task of the teacher to pass on or transmit an unchanging tradition?
- Or is the process of teaching and learning a 'voyage of discovery' as a result of which student (and teacher) seek to create a world of which they are a part?

Human nature:

- Is the child/student like a bucket into which 'knowledge' is tipped a bit at time?
- Or is the student a 'candle to be lit' rather than a 'bottle to be filled'?

The philosophies which inform a teacher's practice arise from her/his training and experience, and they also help constitute a set of *values* about the educational process which are themselves inextricably part of the teacher – and cannot fail to be transmitted as part of the interaction with pupils and students. They will be evident in the manner in which the teacher conducts the class, in the form of the class, the style of teaching and the strategies employed. They will affect the kinds of relationship between teacher and student.

Over the last few years, there has been pressure to assess teaching using a checklist of skills – the higher the 'score', the better the teacher. This method of accounting does not give attention to those additional elements which are the essence of good teaching.

It is clear that 'good' teachers not only possess competences – the totality of which is more than the sum of the parts – but also that they have the ability to apply them selectively and differentially. This is carried out within a framework of values and relationships in which affective qualities play a vital role. Teaching is not simply about 'delivery' of knowledge and skills, but about *transactions*. There is a moral/ethical dimension in teacher training which must not be lost. The possession of competences is a necessary but not sufficient condition for quality teaching.

"We must not be seduced over the next few years as the competency movement gathers pace . . . into believing that the possession of a certain number or type or range of competences in itself is an accurate or sufficient performance indicator of quality teaching."

Christopher Day (1980), 'Personal Development Planning', *British Journal of In-Service Education*, 20, 3

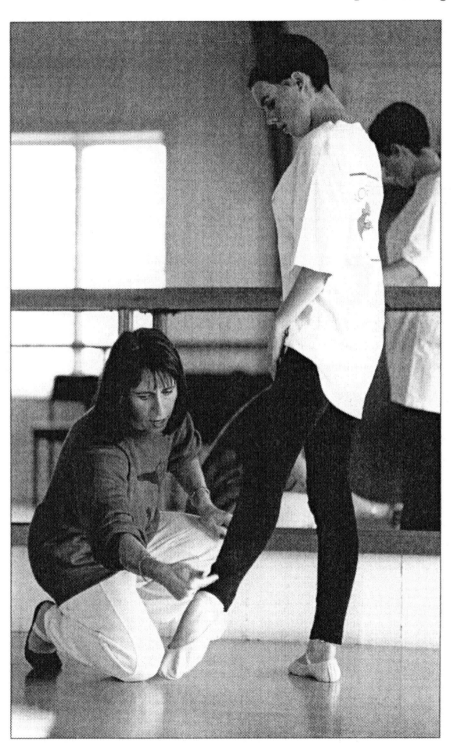

Open ballet class
at Rubicon Dance.
Photo: Richard
Wheeler.

The Student as Learner

When considering how and why students learn, there are some initial questions to be addressed.

Why are they there?

- Have they chosen to come?
- Are they required to attend?
- Are they pleased/reluctant to be there?

What do they hope to gain from the class/workshop/course?

- Technical skill?
- Choreographic expertise?
- Understanding of a dance style?
- The opportunity to dance with others?

How do they see the class/workshop/course?

- As recreation?
- Vocation?
- Social?
- Education?

Who are they?

- Individually, what are the ages, sex, background, experience, understanding of dance?
- What is the composition of the group as a whole?

Towards a Philosophy of Teaching and Learning

The following statements give the essence of views which I hold dearly, and I would like to think that they are evident in my work.

- Everyone can dance – and is entitled to dance.
- Teaching is more than just the transmission of knowledge and skills.
- The role of the student is not just a passive one of simply receiving, but one in which active contribution is valued.

Method of Work

- The 'dance as art' model – *compose, perform, appreciate* – provides a framework for planning and working.
- It is important to make clear the aims and structure of the dance class to ensure confidence and security for both teacher and student, as well as to enhance opportunities for creativity.
- The dance class should not be an embarrassing, exposing experience, but rather an enlivening, invigorating one.
- In order to establish an effective learning environment, it is necessary to consider different leadership roles, teaching styles and strategies.
- The method of presentation should be such as to encourage the gradual transfer of ownership of the work from teacher to student.

Defining Good Practice

"We are what we repeatedly do.
Excellence, then, is not an act – but a habit."
Aristotle

What do I look for in good teaching?

• Energy, enthusiasm, knowledge and expertise which is communicated to students in order to stimulate, challenge, provoke and encourage them to reach their full potential.
• A safe setting for creativity and spontaneity to flourish and develop.
• An environment which encourages mutual respect and support for all the participants.

I asked for the views of several colleagues with much experience – Chris Thomson (director of Education and Community Programmes, Contemporary Dance Trust), Ruth Till (director of Rubicon Dance), Veronica Jobbins (senior lecturer, Laban Centre, and Chair of the NDTA), and Jane Mooney (Director, Suffolk Dance Agency). Some of the personal qualities they look for are:

• Honesty.
• Freshness.
• Reliability.
• A sense of humour.
• Consistency.
• Perceptiveness.
• Imagination.
• Creativity.

Chris thinks that teachers should have a feeling for the aesthetic dimension of dance. Jane suggests that for students to reach their full potential as artists, they need to be able to express movement with proficiency: 'Good teaching connects creativity to technique and technique to creativity.'

They were unanimous in identifying the 'ability to inspire confidence':

Rubicon Dance:
integrated primary
schools project.
Photo: Richard
Wheeler.

- Someone able to get the best out of people.
- Someone who wants to be there.
- An expectation that they will not give anything less than their best.
- Demanding the highest standards and quality which are achievable.
- Ability to generate enthusiasm. This is developed also by sensing and responding to individual needs and nurturing each individual.
- Have the welfare of students at heart.
- Start where they the students are.
- Respect the students as individuals, each with something to offer.
- Instil a sense of group, as well as individual, awareness.
- Build a team working towards the common goal.

Ruth pointed out that, in many community contexts, the word 'teacher' is not appropriate. The titles of 'dance development leader' or 'dance development worker' tend to be used. These more accurately describe the kind of work and the methodology which applies: that of being a facilitator. Adaptability and a variety of leadership skills are vital to be able to deal with the diverse community needs.

It is necessary to be aware of the background and culture of the students. This will affect the form of the dance class and the choice of material, kinds of accompaniment, the method of presentation and strategies to be used.

These features will not be present without careful and thorough planning. This will allow for flexibility. Absence of planning leads to rigidity and places limitations on possibilities. Work should be carefully structured but the structure should not be a straitjacket but maintain 'a balance between control and freedom'. To be creative requires safe discipline yet freedom to create.

Understanding of the context was of particular concern. Veronica talked about the school setting where dance is an educational activity and contributes to the whole curriculum. She expressed the view that it is necessary in this situation to be first a good *teacher*, and then a good *dance* teacher. Subject knowledge is important, but more important is the ability to engage children in the activity of dancing. Progress may be slow, and so learning dance should be seen as a continuum, a journey of development. The teacher should have an awareness and understanding of the management structure and internal politics of the school.

They looked for 'good relationships' – wider than just the context of the dance class. Ruth stressed the need for the community dance teacher not only to be able to generate interest in dance for the participants but also to engage all the support staff – administrators, caretakers, leaders. Veronica similarly argued that teachers should have a good working relationship with colleagues in the school.

An interesting question arises from these observations: are different qualities required of teachers in different contexts, or is it more to do with how they are applied?

Jane was concerned that the teacher should establish a culture in which feedback is not only welcomed but actively sought. There should be an acknowledged process between teacher and students of asking questions, reflecting back, repeating and extending, confirming and affirming through feedback. This is based on the appreciation that a 'good experience' is not enough for development. Only when it is extended into a more conscious realisation of what has been gained, what new competency has been acquired, is the student able, at a later date, to utilise it in an enhanced manner.

Amongst teachers' behaviour they disliked were:

- Being unmusical.
- Unfair comment, empty praise.
- Dangerous tasks.
- Enjoying the class more than the students.

However, the main thing these colleagues deplored in teaching was a *lack of professionalism*. They pointed to:

- Inadequate preparation.
- The use of inappropriate material.
- A negative manner.
- Not correcting enough.
- Poor use of voice and language.
- Egotism.
- Showing off.
- Being late.

- Not having tapes set.
- Over-sensitivity to feedback.
- Lack of interest in self-evaluation.

'Good' and 'Bad' Teaching

Sometimes, when taking workshops concerned with teaching and learning, I ask the participants to consider good and bad examples of teaching and their effects. I ask everyone to remember a 'good' teacher – someone who was particularly inspiring, who made a strong impression on them. What was it about them that had this effect? What were the particular characteristics of the teacher? I ask them to think of words, phrases, which express their qualities and then, in groups, to share these thoughts and write them up on large sheets of paper. Typical comments about 'good' teachers are:

- Enthusiastic.
- Supportive.
- Knowledgeable.
- Well-prepared.
- Sense of humour.
- Actively involved.
- Gives praise.
- Concerned with individuals.
- Shows respect.

These are then considered and discussed. Participants are then asked to follow the same procedure and think about a 'bad' teacher – someone about whom they have negative feelings; whose classes they hated. Again, they are asked to think of words to describe this teacher. This time, I tend to get responses like:

- Sarcastic.
- Lazy.
- Not prepared.

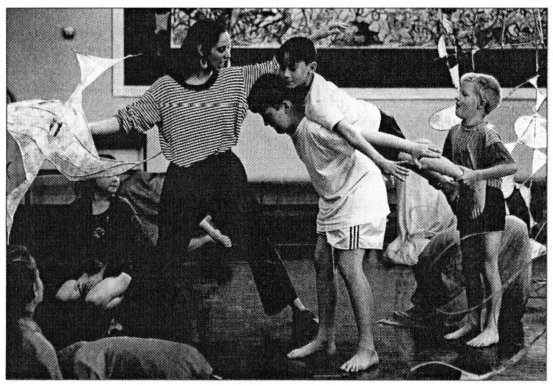

Photo: Adam Eastland. Contemporary Dance Trust.

- Inconsistent.
- Narcissistic.
- Has favourites.
- Destructive.
- Dull.
- Boring.

Engaging Students in the Activity

It becomes very obvious from these workshops what are perceived as the positive and negative characteristics of teachers and how they influence the learning process. We know that a good teacher can capture and retain students' interest, while a bad or poor teacher can turn students off and get in the way of their learning. Perhaps it is worth analysing ourselves as teachers, and reflecting upon our personal qualities. We would all like to think that we fall into the 'good' category', but if we are honest we should acknowledge our weaknesses as well as our strengths, and work to improve them.

We sometimes have to work very hard to motivate ourselves as teachers to be fully engaged in the present, for example when:

- We are not feeling 100 per cent fit.
- The working conditions are poor.
- The students are uncooperative.

But in fact, in circumstances like these, we need to be *more* motivated and be prepared to work much harder than usual to achieve student involvement.

How can we actively engage our students in a positive learning environment? How can

Parents and toddlers class, Suffolk Dance. Photo: Mike Kwasniak.

we make them want to do it; to be there? I think that it is very much to do with gaining and retaining respect for each other. The first encounter – how the teacher begins – is crucial. It is important quickly to establish a sense of community within the group, in which everyone is valued – the students by the teacher, the teacher by the students, and the students by each other. The teacher has to create an atmosphere in which the individual is able to make a contribution and the students are able to appreciate the knowledge, skills, and in some cases the authority of the teacher.

It could be productive to discuss your expectations as a teacher and to consider those of the students and how they might be achieved. It could be helpful to negotiate together to establish ground rules about what is and what is not acceptable. These could be to do with issues such as suitable clothing, not chewing in class, warming up, and so on.

Knowing each other's names is an important step to effective dialogue. As the teacher becomes more familiar with the group, s/he will be able to recognise the strengths and weaknesses of each student. Good teaching is about good observation, about sensing what is needed and responding appropriately.

There are times when the reasons for the lack of success may not be entirely our fault. Circumstances may be against us, for example:

- If the information about the ability and experience of the group was misleading.
- The students may be undisciplined or unmotivated.
- The group might include a difficult individual who demands special attention.

It may take a long period of time to gain the group's respect and confidence and achieve good results.

Beginning with Ourselves

It might be productive, in evaluating our effectiveness as teachers, to consider how we appear to our students. It is not enough just to plan interesting and challenging material (although this is essential); the way in which it is presented and how we communicate have a significant influence on the success of the class.

Although it is important to be honest with ourselves – to be who we are and not try to imitate someone else – we should also be aware that the ways we speak, move and otherwise present ourselves affect our students. We need to consider how our tone of voice and body language may convey a positive or negative attitude, which will be transmitted to our students. Effective teaching requires active participation and commitment by the teacher. This is shown by the way in which the teacher demonstrates alertness and energy in both oral and body language. A teacher who uses language effectively and imaginatively, and who uses movement skilfully and expressively, can provoke, encourage and enthuse students to engage with the activity.

Good observation helps us to be aware of our students' strengths and weaknesses, of when they are making progress and when they are not. The skills of communication allow us to be able to anticipate and respond to students' needs and to offer critiques and/or encouragement as appropriate.

Management is an essential element of good teaching. This includes such things as communication and organisation, for example:

- How the ideas and movement material are presented.
- How the involvement of the students in the process is maintained.
- The way in which the teacher organises the time during the class, paces the work, and gives a sense of building to a conclusion.

It is through the acquisition of such knowledge and skills that the good dance teacher is able to engage the minds, bodies and spirits of the students.

Learning Styles

The more we understand about how we learn, the more effective we are likely to be as teachers. In *Beginning with Ourselves* (1987) David E. Hunt examines what he calls 'learning style'; how a person receives and transmits information. He argues that, as teachers, we need to match our approach to teaching to the needs of our students. We should be able to adapt to approaching different classes in different ways. Hunt suggests that we informally assess the learning of others as we communicate with them and match our communication with this informal assessment. He sees this process in two parts. It begins with the teacher reading or assessing the situation and then responding to it. Teachers are constantly doing this shifting and adjusting anyway, but may not have formally given it attention.

The steps involved in the process can be viewed as *if* and *then*: '*if* this is the case, *then* I need to . . .' Hunt describes this as 'matching the moment'. Becoming aware of this is the first step in demystifying the idea of learning style.

Now we are going to make a formal attempt to capture the intuitive implicit process that is part of effective communication in teaching.

The Teacher as Student

Consider yourself in the role of student and how you learn. Think about a past learning experience, involving your work or a recreational activity. Pick out one that was a good learning experience. Write down its characteristics in a word or phrase. Repeat the procedure for a negative or poor learning experience. What made it so? Now look back at what you have observed about the two contrasting experiences and see if you can go further in identifying the most important differences. You might find it useful if you get some colleagues to carry out this exercise, and then to share your thoughts.

Try completing the following:

- The best way for me to learn is . . .
- I learn best when . . .
- I have trouble learning when . . .
- The following things get in the way of learning . . .

Teachers at a workshop gave the following replies to 'I learn best when . . .':

I feel safe . . . trusted . . . recognised . . . curious . . . interested . . . motivated . . . allowed to be an individual . . . when the work was relevant . . . connected to my experience . . . when there was order and clarity . . . when I was impressed with the teacher's knowledge, skill, conviction . . . when the group dynamics worked well . . . when I was feeling confident, on top of the material, fresh, active, fit . . .

Replies to 'I have trouble learning when . . .' included:

I feel insecure . . . uncomfortable . . . lacking in confidence . . . demoralised . . . when the material is inappropriate . . . irrelevant . . . when the teacher is unprepared . . . has no conviction . . . no passion or vision . . . when work is rushed . . . no time to go in depth or to fully understand before moving on . . . when the space is crowded . . . when the atmosphere is hostile . . . when there is undue competition . . . when I feel tired . . . depressed . . . dispersed . . . unmotivated . . .

Going back to an occasion when your learning was effective and another when you had difficulty in learning, reflect on the part played by the teacher:

• How did the teacher facilitate the students' learning?
• What would have helped the students to have had a more positive experience?

Try to match these two roles – that of the student and that of the teacher.

Motivation

It is evident that people learn best when:

• They are well motivated.
• The work is relevant and meets their needs.
• They are actively involved.
• The atmosphere is conducive to learning.
• They feel respected.

People participate in dance classes for a variety of reasons, some of which are dictated by the context – educational, community, professional, for example. Their motivation for doing so may include some of the following:

• To develop skills.

- To gain knowledge.
- To be creative.
- To express themselves.
- To meet others.
- To gain confidence.
- To get fit.
- 'To see if I can'.
- To work with others.
- To feel better.

Motivating Factors

There may be times when some individuals feel discouraged and lacking in motivation. This might be due to poor working conditions. Students tend not to be motivated when:

- The space is too large/too small.
- There are too few/too many students.
- The floor is cold/dirty/splintered/unsprung.
- The room is too hot/too cold.

If the group dynamics are not good, this can also lead to a lack of motivation. This may be a result of:

- Individuals bringing negative attitudes (which may have nothing to do with the class).
- Conflicting factions within the class.
- Individuals who demand constant attention.

The way in which the teacher deals with these negative factors is crucial. For example, it might be possible to make changes to the work space. Changing attitudes of students might be more difficult. They are more likely to respond to a teacher who demonstrates positive motivating factors – such as their commitment, enthusiasm, and passion for the subject – and to a teacher who shows genuine concern for their success and achievement.

Students tend to feel motivated when:

- The work is meaningful, interesting and varied.
- They are given realistic challenges and goals.
- They feel part of the process.
- They have some measure of responsibility, of decision-making.
- They are given recognition, respect.
- They have a sense of growth and personal development.

Equal Opportunities

Equal opportunity is about ensuring the right that everyone can dance and is entitled to dance. We need to consider how we can contribute to making this happen. Whether we work on our own or for an institution – community centre, dance company, and so on – we need to be certain that everything possible is done to make dance accessible and not exclusive. If you work for an organisation, check the equal opportunities policy. As teachers, we transmit attitudes and values in our work. This is evident in the way we use language and express ourselves, the views we hold, the selections we make, what we think is important. We have a responsibility to challenge prejudice and inequality.

Demonstrate your commitment to equal opportunities through everything you do and say in your work. Consider what attitudes, knowledge and values you have about those you teach. What expectations do you have about their habits, customs, interests, behaviour, and so on? Do you respond differently to those of different age, sex, race, sexual orientation? Try to give everyone equal worth. Value your students' individuality and treat them with respect. Foster this kind of relationship within the group. Do not expect that because people in a group have something in common that they are all alike and will have the same views and interests. Discourage negative statements and stereotypical remarks. We can all think of occasions when groups are categorised in this way; for example, as I get older, it irritates me when assumptions are made about my age group.

Give Boys a Chance

Traditionally 'dance as art', as an expression of feelings, has been seen as a feminine activity – the province of girls. And so boys who dance are not considered masculine.

This is not the case in certain social settings, where it is safe to dance. In these circumstances the environment allows the male to be part of the group, while at the same time encouraging individual self-expression. But when dance is seen as art or as part of education, negative attitudes come into play. Homophobic attitudes to homosexuality dictate that macho man doesn't dance.

While it is not possible for the dance teacher to change the view of society regarding men and dance, within the dance class s/he can work on negative attitudes. It is necessary to provide an environment where boys can express themselves and become familiar with the art form without feeling threatened or embarrassed. The importance of male role models should not be underestimated. Opportunities should be found for boys *and* girls to encounter male teachers and professional dancers.

Some teachers have tried to solve the problem of resistance by presenting boys with movement material that expresses strength or power. In mixed groups, movement material and imagery have been selected with the boys in mind. This is *not* the solution. Although it is important – even essential – to find material for dance that is relevant for boys, this should not be at the expense of the girls. It is dangerous to pander to and reinforce stereotypes. As teachers, we should be challenging them and breaking down prejudice. Everyone – male and female – should be entitled to express him or herself, using the fullest range of movement vocabulary: *both* men and women can be sensitive, strong, aggressive, delicate . . .

Cultural Diversity

Throughout the world, people dance to express themselves, and have done so for thousands of years. This happens in a range of contexts and takes many different forms. Dance, through its expressive and communicative qualities, allows us to be more conscious of ourselves and of the world around us in a unique way. It gives us opportunities to celebrate diversity. It enhances our understanding of the individual, the group, or the community. It strengthens the feeling of belonging.

Try to establish a sense of equality and community in the class, by not making anyone feel excluded or exclusive. Do not to use language or references that have negative overtones or are likely to offend. Do not be restrictive or monocultural in your use of themes and images. Present examples that reflect and value cultural diversity. It is also important to reflect these attitudes in the choice of music used to accompany class. Try to use a wide range of music – not just traditional western – to appeal to all members of the class and so as to extend musical taste. Devise tasks that are meaningful and relevant to the group and their world. Students who do not feel alienated, but are treated with respect and who are given work that has meaning for them, are likely to be confident and motivated.

Body Fascism

Although dance has similarities with other art forms, it is particular in that it involves drawing attention to oneself. The body is the instrument and the means of expression of nonverbal communication. Many people feel anxious about their body image. They think that they are too fat, too thin, that their bottoms are too big, their legs are too short, and so on.

Dance can be very exposing. As teachers we need to be sensitive to students' anxieties about their bodies and to discover ways of encouraging them to have a more positive body image. There has been a tradition in the professional dance world towards *body fascism*: an idea that dancers have to be a particular size, shape, height and weight and ethnic origin. The pressure to conform has sometimes led to eating disorders and other psychological problems. Despite some movements to the contrary, this tradition of what a dancer should look like is still evident in some places. We must be careful not to promote such attitudes in our classes.

Some people can feel particularly exposed and vulnerable in the dance class. For instance, puberty is a difficult time for many young people. Some may wish to 'cover up' to hide the changes that are in progress in their bodies. They feel most comfortable in large baggy clothing. Don't see this as a problem. As they gain confidence, they can be encouraged to discard some of the layers.

Rubicon Dance in Romania, integrated project with deaf and disabled children. Photo: Eric Hands.

Clothes and Customs

Some ethnic groups, for example Sikh men or Muslim women, may have strict dress codes to which they adhere. This should not be seen as a problem but as perfectly legitimate.

Dance clothes worn by some members of the group might be influenced by current fashion trends. Attention should not be drawn to those unable to follow these for, perhaps, financial reasons. Comfortable, loose clothes should be acceptable in most dance settings.

There are contexts where the traditional leotards and tights are regulation and are absolutely right and appropriate. Explain why it is important to be able to see how the body is functioning, to be able to discern correct alignment and placement, where the movement is initiated, clarity of line, and so on.

Body Contact

Dancing together requires a degree of sensitivity in terms of personal space, proximity, body contact and touch. If you sometimes use touch to clarify a personal correction when teaching, it would be wise to have explained the reason for doing this to the class when first meeting them. This would allow any student who might feel this practice unacceptable to say so. This could apply to students from cultures where, traditionally, members of the opposite sex do not touch in public. In most cases, however, body contact, supporting, lifting and taking each others' weight can be liberating rather than threatening experiences.

Special Needs

Think of ways to organise your class to take account of any of your students with special needs. Consider ways that both you and your students can accommodate such individuals. Differentiation of task should be considered – giving students different tasks which are demanding and achievable for them. I have had the experience of teaching visually and hearing impaired students and students with limited mobility in wheelchairs in classes with able-bodied students. I found this to be a tough challenge. I quickly realised that to ask disabled students 'Just do what you can' is not good enough. I tried a number of methods of involving such students, some more successful than others. The task is to challenge students with special needs – as much as the able-bodied – to explore new ways to move.

2

Planning a Dance Course

Key elements when planning a dance course are:

- Knowing your students.
- Aims and objectives.
- Course content.
- Teaching methods.
- Assessment.
- Evaluation.

Knowing Your Students

Planning a dance course should start with a needs analysis. It is important to have some advance knowledge of a group before teaching them. What do you know about the numbers involved, age, sex, experience, level of skill, special needs, cultural and ethnic background of the students? What are their aspirations and expectations? A good needs analysis form, with information completed by the students or someone setting up the course, can be invaluable for the teacher. Having access to at least some of this information should enable the teacher to determine the concepts, knowledge and skills to be explored.

Photo: Adam Eastland. Contemporary Dance Trust.

The *aims* and *content* of the course may have been set out before you joined the project. The course may have a clearly defined syllabus, such as published curricular guidelines as a part of the National Curriculum, or a Royal Academy of Dancing examination syllabus. Although the course content is prescribed, it will be necessary, in your planning, to take account of individual needs of students and personal objectives. A number of ways in which you might identify their needs might include:

• Talking to someone who has worked with them before.
• Talking to other experienced teachers who have worked with similar groups.

However, try not to have too many preconceived ideas (assumptions can be made about, say, a group of urban teenagers or an over-fifties women's group which could be found to be entirely wrong). After finding out as much as you can, be prepared to trust your own judgement and plan accordingly, but be open to modifying your plan if necessary.

Aims and Objectives

Aims are general statements of intent giving the overall purpose of the course. They are long term and may be difficult to evaluate, for example:

- To work towards increased strength, flexibility and coordination.
- To facilitate movement invention.
- To encourage students to be imaginative, inventive and provocative in their selection of movement material.

Objectives are specific action statements setting out what the students should achieve as a result of the course. They are quantifiable, and can be evaluated, for example:

- To gain skill in the transference of weight.
- To show understanding of *motif* and *development*.
- To demonstrate the ability to analyse a dance work with particular reference to its historical context.

Objectives should be SMART:

- **S**pecific.
- **M**easurable.
- **A**chievable.
- **R**ealistic.
- **T**ime bound.

Course Content

Account should be given to adequate preparation time to allow you to plan the content and structure of the class or series of classes. It is important to establish clear aims and objectives, and to ensure that there be logical progression within the class and from one class to the next. The choice of material should not be haphazard or capricious, but should be determined by the application of valid criteria. Being well prepared gives a sense of security to the teacher and the students. Students are entitled to a well prepared class.

Before getting down to the detail of the content, you will need to be clear as to the overall purpose of the course (aims) and how you would describe it in general terms. Then begin to explore it in more precise terms by taking account of what you intend your students to achieve (objectives). You should identify the knowledge, skills and concepts they will need to have grasped before they can move on, and the steps you will need to take for them to reach that achievement. This should help you decide the nature and quantity of the material to be covered overall and in an individual class.

Being well prepared does not mean that a plan must be rigidly adhered to. It is good to prepare more material than you might need – but do not over-teach. Resist the temptation to teach everything you know. While it is important to keep students interested and challenged, they need time to absorb and consolidate material. Consider a number of outcomes – such as possible changes of direction and/or different finishing points – to take account of students' needs.

Offer movement experiences which are suitable for the group, taking account of differing requirements such as experience, age, sex. Any themes and images chosen should appeal and be relevant to the participants.

The Structure of a Creative Dance Class

The structure I follow uses strands of the 'dance as art' model:

- Compose.
- Perform.
- Appreciate.

Not all these strands need to be included or given equal importance in each class, but students should be given opportunity to encounter all three. Depending on the age, experience and level of understanding, the strands can be considered in simple or more complex forms, such as:

- Make, do, show.
- Compose, dance, discuss.
- Choreograph, perform, analyse.

This way of working helps to develop articulate dancers. The uniqueness of dance is that the body is the instrument of expression and the medium is movement. We all have personal ways of moving with which we feel comfortable. These might be expansive, gestural, using large amounts of space, stable, controlled, or giving into weight. The dance teacher's job is not to confine students to copying the teacher's movement preferences but to give them the opportunity, through exploration, to extend their repertoire of movement and expressive skills. They are then enabled to communicate ideas, feelings and sensations more effectively.

The method that follows is not the only or the definitive way to structure a creative dance class, but it is a method that the author has tried and tested on many occasions with a variety of groups in different contexts.

Clarity of intention is important, and intentions need to be made explicit. Right from the beginning, from the warm up through to the dance conclusion, the movement aims lead the direction of the class. This gives everyone involved a clear understanding of the identity of the material to be explored, and equips them to evaluate the effectiveness of the process.

The logicality of the structure gives security to the teacher and the students. However it does not have to be rigidly adhered to. Good teaching requires responding to students' needs. If the teacher overestimates or underestimates the ability of the students, s/he will have to consider how to proceed and what adjustments to make. Students may provide more interesting ways to develop material than had been planned. Flexibility is necessary so that the teacher can take advantage of such changes of direction.

This method is not about 'anything goes' but about giving people a unique way of expressing themselves. The teacher must find ways to engage the minds, bodies and spirits of the dancers by being rigorous and demanding. Tasks should be increasingly challenging

Junior summertime dance at Suffolk Dance. Photo: Mike Kwasniak.

and should not allow students to fall back on to familiar movement patterns, but should require them to struggle to find new ways in which to move.

The following headings are useful in planning the structure of a class:

- Movement aims – intention of the class.
- Introduction and warm up – preparing the body, engaging the mind.
- Exploration and development – new ways of moving, forming phrases of movement.
- Dance – composing.
- Appreciation and evaluation- observing, analysing, reflecting.

Movement Aims

What aspects of movement, selected from the body of knowledge, are to be explored? What other ideas/themes/images are to be used to highlight and colour the work? The choices made will depend upon:

- The knowledge of the group.
- Their interests and expectations.
- The level of their experience, skill and understanding.

Some questions to consider:

- What have they done before?
- Should it continue?
- Do they need to move on to a new aspect of movement?
- What have they not encountered?
- What have they not mastered?

Learning to dance is more a cyclical experience than a linear one, in terms of progression. Material should be revisited, concepts reintroduced, skills re-encountered in order to give students the opportunity to reinforce understanding and to widen and deepen their knowledge.

The way in which a class begins can crucially affect its success. It should encompass a philosophy that everyone can dance, all can contribute and feel valued. Students should feel secure in a non-competitive environment.

The introduction should clearly define the aims and objectives of the class. The warm up material should reflect these and not be concerned with something different and separate from the rest of the work. The warm up should establish body and mind concentration. Activities should involve awareness of self, of the space, of the teacher, and of each other. It should include some whole-body exercises as well as work on individual body parts, some travelling in the dance space, and awareness of others.

Activities should be consistent with safe body management. Attention should be given to good alignment and posture. It is important that the warm-up adequately prepares students for the demands of whatever is to follow. By the end of the warm up, the teacher needs to have established a positive working atmosphere in which each individual is centred, focused and ready to apply the skills experienced.

Exploration and Development

Exploration is to do with problem-solving. Depending on the nature of the tasks, the students may be required to work on their own or with others. The tasks lead them from what they know to what is unfamiliar. The challenge is, through improvising, to:

- Find new solutions to movement problems.
- Extend their movement vocabulary.
- Consider new combinations of movement.

Development is concerned with extending movement skills by making selections from the improvised material and making phrases of movement which can be repeated, refined and perfected.

Dance

Drawing on the improvised experiences and the phrases of movement, students can start to *compose* dance – either independently or with others. It is the nature of the task that will

London Contemporary Dance Theatre workshop. Photo: Philip Polglaze.

determine whether it will be an individual or a group process. Forming a dance, however slight, can give a sense of achievement. In the early stages, students may produce short, simple phrases of movement, whereas more experienced ones can be given more complex tasks with specific choreographic demands.

Appreciation and Evaluation

Opportunity should be given to reflect upon the aims and objectives of the class and the work covered. This should be a continual process which takes place throughout the class. It may be done by showing each other's work and observing and commenting on it. This will only be effective if the activities are treated with respect by both the dancers and the viewers.

The level of sophistication in both performance and analytical skills will vary depending upon the age, skill and experience of the participants. However, emphasis should be given to both appreciation and evaluation throughout the lesson and not merely dealt with at the end. They can be achieved in a variety of ways, for example:

- Asking questions.
- Showing examples.
- Discussing solutions.

Structure of a Lesson – An Example

Dance Styles: Tango

Movement Aims: Action/dynamics relationship

Music: Man Jumping, 'The Perils of Tourism' from *World Service*; 'Adios Muchachos' and 'Yira Yira' by Florindo Sessone, from the compilation CD *Buenos Aires By Night*

Warm-Up:

- Open and close with the breath.
- Small movements from the centre, becoming more expansive. Horizontal, vertical, diagonal into a balance. Changes of size and changes of time – expansive, staccato. Imagine how the bellows of an accordion expand and contract.
- Travelling through space.

Exploration:

- Gesture hip(s), torso, shoulder(s) – small, larger, large.
- Rush through space, stop, hold, look, retreat – forward, backward, sideways. Add step pattern to include changes of speed.
- Turn, open closed, spiral, series of turns – spotting, speeding up, slowing down.

'Dance Blaze' 98
at Suffolk Dance.
Photo: Mike
Kwasniak.

Development:

Develop a phrase which includes: large expansive movement, gesture, travel step pattern, turn. In any order to include strong use of focus, moment of stillness, changes of speed and direction.

Dance:

With a partner, combine material including body contact and same use of focus listen to the form of the music.

Appreciation and Evaluation:

Draw attention to the variety of ways in which individuals have responded to the tasks. Show duets. Discuss how effectively *dynamics* and *relationship* have been used.

Teaching Methods

No one method of work is right for every situation. The teacher needs to be creative, flexible, and to consider a range of teaching styles and strategies to enable students to learn. The method of teaching should take account of:

- What is the subject matter? Which style is most appropriate?
- Who are the students? How will they best learn?

Below are a number of styles which can be employed in teaching dance. Although one style might predominate through the session, more than one might be used to enable students to learn more effectively.

- Demonstration.
- Individual practice.
- Problem-solving.

- Collaboration.

They are covered in some detail in *In Touch With Dance* (Gough, 1995).

Demonstration

The teacher has the knowledge and skills and the student learns by observing, copying and applying the information.

- You must be able to demonstrate well and break the material down into manageable amounts.
- Be sure that you can be seen as well as heard. Change your position and that of your students.
- Use descriptive language to assist your demonstration.
- Encourage people to ask questions to help them understand.
- Ask students to check one another.
- Do not move on too quickly before people have mastered the material well enough.
- Try to increase the level of challenge and complexity to give a sense of achievement.

Demonstration increases students'

- Observational skills.
- Ability to translate observed movement into their own bodies.
- Ability to copy accurately.
- Ability to become more skilful.

Individual Practice

The teacher sets the task and supervises the students who learn by individual practice.

- The students are given responsibility for their own learning, by being given time to try out the task and make improvements.

- The task must be clear.
- The teacher is able to observe individuals and give support and encouragement.
- Help needs to be specific and precise.
- Guard against giving too much attention to particular individuals at the expense of others.
- Draw attention to examples of good practice.
- Be encouraging and give praise to achievement.
- Avoid competition.
- Students could work with a partner and give each other corrections.

Individual practice gives opportunity for students to:

- Understand and analyse a task accurately.
- Extend their movement memory.
- Work in a disciplined manner.
- Be aware of their own strengths and weaknesses.

Problem-Solving

This method usually begins with the teacher (or teacher and students jointly) posing a question, setting a task for which the student has to find a solution. It is necessary that:

- The demands of the task are clearly set out.
- The teacher observes student responses and acts as advisor when appropriate.
- Students should be prepared to work deeply and not accept easy solutions.
- They are encouraged to consider unfamiliar movement material and ways of working.

Problem solving encourages:

- Individuality,
- Students to work in unfamiliar ways,
- Decision-making,
- A process of learning from enquiry to solution.

Collaboration

This approach invites cooperation through working collaboratively with others. The teacher's role as a facilitator is to:

- Create an atmosphere where everyone can participate and interaction is valued.
- Decide on the composition of the group. Is it to be free-for-all, or do you want to arrange people in particular ways?
- Ensure students are well prepared and are able to contribute to the task.
- Monitor the work by moving around the room – listening, observing and encouraging
- persuade students to keep on task, not to spend too long talking rather than doing (the larger the group, the more time they will need).
- Give time after completion to evaluate the task.

Collaboration gives students the experience of:

- Working closely with others in a joint venture.
- Learning both from and with others.
- Extending negotiating and appreciation skills.

Whichever style is chosen, students should be encouraged to be responsible for their own learning. The role of the teacher is gradually to allow the ownership of the work to become that of the students.

In addition to styles of presentation there are a number of approaches and strategies that can be employed depending on the nature of the students and their particular needs.

Some Things to Bear in Mind

- Are they an established group who know each other?
- What have they done before?
- What was particularly successful? This does not mean that you should do something similar, but could indicate the direction to take.

- Is this the first time the class have met? If so it will require a very different approach from that of a group who are familiar with dance and each other.

Asking Questions

Questions are one way to get people thinking and involved. They can be a valuable way to stimulate interest and encourage people to participate. They can evoke physical and sensory responses as well as intellectual ones. Questions can aid communication between teacher and students, Everyone can be involved. Considering the question is often more important than the answer.

Keeping people actively engaged may involve changing the level or pace of the class to recognise and value individual needs and differences. Students may not respond positively to material that is either too difficult or not challenging enough. Both of these conditions can occur in the same class and will require the teacher to be open and flexible to change in order to be able to deal with them.

Example of a Lesson Plan using a Different Styles and Strategies

Movement Aims: Action and relationship
Stimulus: Dance styles

Warm up
Travel forward 2 3, and back 2 3, skimming the floor.
Travel forward 2 3, and back 2 3, turn 2 3, turn 2 3. *Demonstration*

Using these directions add a step pattern of your own.
e.g. chassé forward 2 3, chassé back 2 3,
step hop hop turning, step hop hop turning. *Problem-solving*

Devise a phrase which you can perfect and perform well. *Individual practice*

Divide the class. Group A observes while group B shows their sequences. Members of group A join in when they see an interesting example they which to copy. Change groups over.

Demonstration

Exploration and development:
Taught section.
Chassé to the right 2 steps, and the left 2 steps.
Lean to the right and left, full turn to the right.
Repeat sequence on the left.
Take right foot behind, step to side with left, take right across, kick with left.
Repeat with left foot leading.
Take 4 steps forward and across, beginning with the right foot.
Jump and bend on the right and left.
4 steps forward.

Demonstration

Make the material your own so that you can perform it competently.

Individual practice

Try out the sequence using music of a particular style, e.g. jazz.

Problem-solving

Discuss what changed. How did it influence the quality of the movement?

Dance:
In groups of four chose one from a number of given dance styles. e.g. Latin American, Spanish Flamenco, Greek and Russian Folk. Discuss the particular characteristics of the chosen style. Retaining the steps of the taught sequence compose a dance which has some of the essence of the style.

Problem-solving and collaboration

Appreciation and evaluation:
How has the original material changed?
How do the dance styles vary?

For example:

- The size of the movement
- The use of space
- The emphasis on different body parts
- Formation and relationship to others

Criteria for the Unexpected

Try not to be thrown if things do not turn out as you expect; try particularly not to lose your confidence or good humour.

Don't be put off by interruptions. If you keep your concentration and attention on the task in hand, students will quickly retain theirs. If there appear to be problems within a class, do not be afraid to ask what is wrong and to allow people to air their views. If individuals seem to be uncomfortable, anxious or aggressive, find time to discuss their concerns with them individually, quietly, before or after class. Don't ignore them!

Beware of having favourites who get all your attention, or difficult, demanding students who you constantly refer to at the expense of the rest of the class. Some individuals, if they are not fully occupied, may be destructive.

One way of dealing with dominant, aggressive youngsters who demand attention is by giving them some responsibility, such as organising a group or being in charge of the tape or CD player. It can also be helpful to engage anyone sitting out so they can still feel involved in the activity, by giving them observational tasks, such as:

- How did the dancers use the space?
- What moments were memorable?
- How effective were the transitions?

Teachers need to be adaptable. You may find at your first meeting that what you had planned to do is totally inappropriate – not what the student wanted or expected; your expectations are unrealistic and cannot be achieved. You will need to consider ways to proceed. If you encounter reluctance you may get over it by encouraging and persuading students to give your ideas a try. Sometimes a compromise can work, for example by discussing your plans with the group and being prepared to consider any ideas they may contribute. However, there are times when it is better to throw away what you had planned completely. Try to relate to the group and start from a common interest. Find a way to match their interests with the theme or material of the class.

Tracey Brown, Dance Development Officer for Rubicon Dance gave me an example of how she dealt with a reluctant group of male teenagers. In talking about their interests she discovered that one young man did kickboxing. After he had demonstrated some of the moves, the rest of the group showed some enthusiasm and so she used some of the material in a warm up and the movement sequence which followed. She quickly got everyone's attention and they participated well.

There are times in the dance class when it is appropriate for students to be in small groups. This is an important part of dancing. When a group is working well together, it can be a very satisfying experience, providing a supportive, stimulating environment in which all the participants can contribute.

Sometimes the relationships in the group become strained and interaction is difficult. This can happen when a member is domineering, reluctant or difficult to please. In such cases, the teacher needs to intercede to help people to reconsider, to compromise or modify their attitudes to accommodate everyone, in order that the work may proceed.

The teacher's role is that of organiser, facilitator and negotiator. It helps if the task and the time allowed have been clearly set out. The size of the group will determine the amount of time needed to complete the task. With an inexperienced class, it can be helpful also to establish a method of work; that is, the way in which the task is to be completed.

It is necessary, for the teacher and members of the class, to trust and respect each other. This takes time. Success in dance involves hard work, commitment, and a willingness to share and work cooperatively with others. For students to appreciate this and understand the activity they need to become familiar and confident with dance and each other. Don't be disappointed if progress is slow and not always sequential. There may be times when it seems to be at a standstill or to have slipped back. Remember that people learn in different ways and at different rates

Establish and negotiate clear ground rules about what is and what is not acceptable regarding such matters as punctuality, clothing, eating, active participation. If this is done effectively, and all have expressed their expectations clearly, you are less likely to encounter unanticipated problems, because what they can expect of you and you expect of them has been made explicit.

The more experienced you are the less likely you are to be put off by changes, interruptions, demanding individuals, and so on. Much of this is common sense and we usually get better as we become more confident.

Corrections

Corrections should be seen as a positive part of the dance class, when time and attention is given to working more effectively and improving performance. The teacher has to observe students carefully and analyse how best to help them. Students should be prepared to re-examine the task and respond to the teacher's suggestions.

Corrections can indicate ways to:

- Extend skill and deepen understanding.
- Gain greater kinaesthetic awareness.
- Work more safely and efficiently.
- Improve the quality of the movement.

They can be given to all members of the class as general corrections focusing on a common fault or misunderstanding; or they can be personal, where an individual's attention is drawn to ways of improving their performance. Different styles of teaching can be employed when giving corrections, for example:

- Command style. This has been the traditional way that technique classes are taught, so a correction would be given in the form of an instruction – 'Open the chest and extend the movement out beyond the finger tips.'
- Problem-solving. It might be more appropriate in a creative class sometimes to use a problem-solving approach by posing corrections in the form of a question, such as 'Can you find a more effective way to shift your weight from the floor to standing without using your hands?'

Different strategies can be employed when giving corrections, for example:

- Asking the class to watch the teacher perform the task – 'Notice how the turn is initiated by the hip'.
- Concentrating on anatomical detail – 'When you take your arms above your head, take care not to push your ribs forward'.
- Using imagery to illuminate how the movement should feel – its quality. 'Think of skimming the floor, barely touching the surface as you travel'

Attempts should be made to give attention to *all* students, not only the ones who need most help. This may be achieved not in one class but over a series of classes. The focus should be not only on problems but also on praising any improvement and achievement. After giving a correction, make sure that your students are given the opportunity to apply it.

Repetition

Repetition is important in the dance class. Students need to feel that they have mastered material sufficiently well before moving on. We can all think of examples where we have not been given enough time to grasp something well enough, and recall the frustration we felt at not succeeding. Equally frustrating is an occasion when an exercise is repeated and repeated until the body cries out to stop, or boredom sets in. Some students do not appreciate the value of repetition, may resist the demand to work more deeply, and have to be persuaded to commit themselves fully to the activity. Repetition is not simply doing the same thing again and getting it right, but is concerned with finding new ways of understanding by exploring the activity as fully as possible and so developing a greater kinaesthetic awareness. To emphasise again:

> "We are what we repeatedly do.
> Excellence, then, is not an act – but a habit."
> Aristotle

Pitching the level of work to give everyone satisfaction and challenge is not easy. Teachers often direct their work at students in the middle range of ability in the class. Inevitably, this leaves the weaker students needing more time and attention and the most able feeling that

Suffolk Dance.
Photo: Mike
Kwasniak.

they are being held back. When working with a group which includes a range of abilities, different strategies may need to be employed to keep everyone alert and actively involved. For example, one might be for more challenge to be given to those members of class who have mastered the material, while attention could then be focused on those who need to give more time to detail in order to consolidate their learning. Another strategy might be for students to join with a partner to check each other's work for accuracy and fluency.

Judging when to move on is difficult. Acute observational skills are demanded of the teacher to decide when it is appropriate.

Making Dance Expressive

"Expression – the memory of things lived."
Madalena Victorino, dance artist, 1997

How can dance be expressive? I was asked this question recently by a student I was teaching. I found it thought-provoking. Although I would like to think that I always try to make dance expressive and to emphasise the quality of the movement, I have not consciously thought how this is achieved. It was salutary, therefore, to be asked to articulate it. We are aware when dance is not expressive: when we see work where little attention is given to the quality, where the dancer simply makes shapes. The movement may be competently per-formed and well-executed, but is meaningless.

Expression is about communicating, making known, defining the intention of the movement. This has to be understood by the dancer and be clear to an observer. It can be as simple as a stretch – but the intention of stretching and all the meaning that the stretch entails must be communicated. We can activate expression by investing the movement with an image, emotion or feeling, such as *tenderness, loneliness, aggression*. The evocative nature of dance enables us to recapture, in the body, such sensations.

Expression begins with the intention – the meaning. It involves the dancers' understand-ing, energy and commitment to make the quality of the movement explicit. For dance to be expressive it needs to be performed with integrity and truth. Expression is:

"Not how people move but what moves them"
Jochen Schmidt, in *Pina Bausch Wuppertal Dance Theatre*, 1987

45

First Encounters

Beginnings are particularly important. They should encompass a philosophy that maintains that everyone can dance, is valued and has a contribution to make. Within a group you will have a variety of people, some of whom may be anxious, resistant, confident or unsure, and so on. It is your job to allay any problems and help them to feel comfortable and part of a supportive group. Students should feel secure in a non-threatening, non-competitive environment. This will assist in establishing a climate conducive to learning.

The way you present yourself as teacher at the first meeting is very important: it sets an expectation and tone for what is to follow. How you use your voice, your verbal and body language will indicate how you are feeling to the class. Try to show confidence even if you do not feel it. If you appear to be enthusiastic and energetic in your language and movement this will encourage your students to become involved. It is necessary to gain their attention quickly and establish your competence as a teacher.

The way you begin a class can crucially affect its success, but there are some things which should be considered first before beginning the class:

- Injuries and medical problems.
- Safety.
- Environment/space.
- Clothing.
- Jewellery.

As far as is possible, you should follow recognised administration and organisational procedures that have been established in the school or centre where you are going to work.

Injuries and Medical Problems

As a teacher, you will need to take account of any medical details or injuries of which you become aware. It is diplomatic to make it possible for individuals with such problems to speak with you privately, rather than in front of the class. You will need to consider if these students will need particular attention and guidance to work safely or, indeed, whether they should participate at all.

Street Beat at Suffolk Dance, August 1998. Photo: Mike Kwasniak.

Safety

Draw attention, in the workplace, to any danger points that may be present, such as hotplates in a school dining hall, tables with sharp corners, slippery floors, and so on. Find out the institutional procedures to deal with injury.

Insurance

It is important that you are adequately insured. Check with the organisations you work for to see if you are covered. You may need to take out a Public Liability Insurance. This area is a regular minefield and you would be wise to obtain some advice about insurance. The

Photo: Adam Eastland. Contemporary Dance Trust.

Foundation for Community Dance has a scheme available to its members – the details are on a leaflet obtainable from the Foundation; and in *Regular Marvels* there is a section on legal matters.

François Matarasso (1994), *Regular Marvels*, Community Dance and Mime Foundation

Clothing

As discussed in the section on equal opportunities, the kind of clothing worn may be dictated by the context. If you require particular kinds of clothing to be worn, explain why. These reasons should be functional rather than cosmetic. It may be that some students will not wish to conform to usual dancewear, because of cultural differences. Normally, this is acceptable and should not be seen as a problem. You may have to encourage students to work with bare feet. Explain that the feet can be more steady and articulate without shoes. In some circumstances trainers may be acceptable.

Jewellery

You should require students to remove jewellery and explain the safety implications for doing so. It would be helpful if you had some suitable container available in which such objects could be safely placed until the class finishes.

The Dance Environment

Try to arrive early – or make a preliminary visit – to familiarise yourself with the dance space and any equipment to be used. Get to know any members of staff – teaching, administrative and domestic. The initial response of a class may be influenced by certain conditions over which the teacher has little or no control, but of which s/he will need to take account. For instance, the mood of the class: Do they appear unsure? Excitable? Lethargic? Do they know you? Each other? What have they been doing immediately prior to the class? Is it the first class of the day? Or is it after a hard day's work? Students may be affected by the temperature and weather conditions, such as extremes of heat or cold. Small children seem to become wild in windy conditions! Is the dance space a warm, clean, attractive, safe environment? Is the floor well sprung, with a smooth surface? The teacher will need quickly to assess the mood of the group, the conditions of the workplace, and respond appropriately.

Starting Class

Do you begin at the scheduled time if there is only a handful of people present? I suggest you wait until the majority have arrived, but make it clear to the group that you intend to start on time in the future. Explain why people who arrive late may not be able to join, for reasons of safety, if they have missed the warming up. Depending on the context, the teacher might respond differently to latecomers: in a school or college setting, punctuality could be expected of students, while for members of a community class a more flexible attitude to timekeeping might apply.

Begin by trying to establish a non-threatening environment through dialogue with the members of the class. If you intend to take a few minutes to do so, suggest the group sit down rather than stand. A circle may be a suitable intimate gathering for a small group. However, it can be inhibiting: as everyone can be seen, some may find it initially exposing. Whatever the shape of the group, make sure that you have eye contact with everyone. Notice anyone who places themselves outside the group or is unwilling or unable to give eye contact. They may need some nurturing, but be cautious about drawing attention to them.

Introduce yourself – giving a short account of your relevant background and experience – and ask the students to do the same. You may want to find out more about them, but keep this short. There may be times later in class or at the end when you can continue the discussion. It is important to acknowledge their background and experience.

It is essential that you learn the names of your students. There are a number of ways to help recall names. One is to jot down on a register or list some characteristic that might help you recognise a student. During the class, find ways to learn names, for example by using some name games in the warm up. Once students have left class, look at your list to see how many names you can remember. Before the next class, do the same. By the end of the second class you should know everyone's name. After that, it is too embarrassing to ask.

Workshop with deaf children in Romania, with Rubicon Dance. Photo: Eric Hands.

You are nearly ready to start to move; but first, briefly explain your aims and objectives. So if the class you have planned is concerned with fall and suspension, explain this to the class. Traditionally, dance teachers have not always verbalised the intention of the class. Doing so gives the work clarity and focus. Students new to dance should also be introduced to the form and structure of a dance class as this will not be familiar to them.

Endings

Just as it is important to begin class on time, it is equally important to finish punctually. Whatever the setting, participants may have pressing commitments and will expect to leave on time. Try not to end abruptly because time is running out. Pace the class so that you have time to round off the work and give a sense of satisfaction and completion.

Time should be given to consolidating knowledge, skills and concepts, so that students can appreciate what they have understood and achieved. Sometimes it is valuable to reflect on the processes encountered and discuss them with the students and listen to their concerns. Part of the conclusion should involve an evaluation, particularly if the session is a 'one-off'. What do they feel about the class? What did they find interesting, valuable? What would they have liked more of – or less of? Offer your evaluation.

If the class is one of a series, confirm any tasks you may have set and/or indicate how they might pursue areas to develop. Thank the participants and say how much you have enjoyed working with them. Give people the opportunity to talk to you individually.

How you end the session and then talk with them informally can motivate them to continue and succeed.

Assessment and Evaluation

These terms are often used interchangeably but perhaps a distinction should be drawn. There is considerable overlap, but – in general – *assessment* considers the extent to which aims and objectives have been achieved, while *evaluation* may be seen as more concerned with *judgements* – about, for example, the effectiveness of the enterprise and whether it is of value (and to whom).

Assessment

By assessing our students' progress and achievement we can:

- Motivate them in the process of learning.
- Sustain their interest by making them aware of how they are doing.
- Identify their capabilities and achievements.
- Consider what should be done next.

The kind of assessment – formal or otherwise – is dependent on the needs of the students and the particular context. It can range from simply observing students in class to a formal examination. As teachers, we are constantly making intuitive judgements about those we teach: have they mastered material sufficiently well to move on or do they need more time to consolidate their learning?

It is crucial that these generalised procedures are supplemented by more specific monitoring and evaluating of individual students. For example, being aware if they are ahead or having difficulty keeping up. This focusing upon particular needs will help determine how to proceed.

Different methods of assessment should be considered depending on the nature of the class and the needs of the students. Some assessment procedures may be already set in place by the institution, the examining board, and so on.

Methods of Assessment:

Diagnostic. Identify strengths and weaknesses. When using this method, try to be as constructive as possible. Be sensitive to the students' shortcomings and draw attention to positive aspects. Find out if the student is able to assess his/her ability. Give clear advice and specific guidelines as to how they should proceed.

Formative. Assess knowledge and skill and provide feedback on how the student is doing. This method should be an integral part of everyday teaching. It is not so much testing as monitoring progress and achievement. It is valuable to take account of students' self-evaluations and to compare these with your assessment of their ability.

Summative. A specially designed assessment procedure to measure the extent of learning over a given period of time, such as a series of workshops, a course, a performance. This kind of assessment tends to be given a higher profile. It should be regarded, however, not only as a final check on achievement, but also as a relevant and a necessary part of the learning/teaching process. The testing should be directly linked to specific learning objectives. This method gives the teacher the opportunity to observe the students ability to, for example:

- Deal with new material.
- Demonstrate particular skills.

Rubicon Dance,
class at Butetown
Youth Dance.
Photo: Richard
Wheeler.

- Master new techniques.
- Identify the strengths and weaknesses of the course.

Assessment procedures should be clear. Students need to be aware of the process and of the criteria for assessment. Whatever the method, they should be encouraged to consider their own ability and aptitudes and to take some responsibility for their own learning.

Evaluation

All art forms are inherently subjective, and subjective evaluations have a legitimate place. These, however, should not be capricious, but founded upon clear perspectives about the nature of dance and dance education.

Whether evaluation needs to be quantitative or qualitative will depend entirely upon the nature of the activity and it would be inappropriate to seek quantitative measures where they do not apply.

In general, quantitative evaluation will take the form of *monitoring* – answering questions such as, How many people were involved? How many sessions took place? Over what period of time? Qualitative evaluation will be useful is seeking to establish whether the activity was seen as worthwhile. This can be a most useful method for challenging, as well as affirming, practice.

The kind of evaluation to be carried out will be directly related to the purpose for which it is done – and for whom. For the participants? For the teachers of the activity? For the institution? Is it for the funding agency?

As with assessment, evaluation may also be either formative or summative.

Such evaluation is best achieved by using a combination of methods:

- Self-evaluation.
- Evaluation by colleagues.
- External evaluation by people recruited specifically for that purpose.

Pressures for accountability in the arts often bring requirements for evaluation. We should be clear, however, about the *purpose* of any evaluation we may undertake. Our major concern should be about improving practice.

> "Most importantly, evaluation is about promoting quality."
> Richard Blanco, dance administrator

Why evaluate? Reasons might be to:

- Establish whether aims and objectives were achieved.
- Identify particular needs.
- Consider community concerns.
- Indicate future development.

For whom is it intended?

- The funder.
- The students.
- The teacher.
- The organiser.

What are we evaluating? What do we hope to learn? What information do we require? You may wish to review:

- The effectiveness of the preparation.
- The appropriateness of the material.
- The expertise of the teacher.
- The satisfaction of participants.
- The quality of outcomes.

When do we evaluate?

Evaluation should not be seen solely as an activity that comes at the end of a course or programme. It needs to be integral to the whole process:

- Identifying needs.
- Preparation and planning.
- Implementation – formative evaluation.
- Conclusion/ reflection – summative evaluation.

Like assessment, the method can range from an informal brief process to a complex, comprehensive one. The choice is dependent upon the purpose. Sometimes a particular project in a school, or perhaps a community setting, will require a particular kind of evaluation. Similarly, a grant from a funding agency might involve specific evaluation of a different type. Whatever the method, it should not be seen as a chore but as a positive opportunity to reflect on our practice. It can promote a dialogue between all the participants involved in a project so that the work can be looked at from the widest perspective. Alternatively, it might have a particular focus on the achievements and aspirations of the students and teacher. The value of the work can be discussed and ways in which it might develop, become more relevant, and so on, can be explored.

"Evaluation is about dialogue; hearing about the experiences of our participants and colleagues. We can reflect and learn from our experiences. It enables a fundamental principle of community dance to be realised – for participants to contribute to the planning and development of community of their work by having a say. It stimulates ideas and allows us to connect our artistic aims with the aspirations of our communities. Through evaluation we keep in touch."
Richard Blanco

While there are traditional methods of evaluating, it is worth considering a range of possibilities and perhaps trying to offer some creative solutions. Examples might be:

- Talk with the class. You may have a general discussion about the workshop/course in which everyone has the opportunity to contribute. This method informs the teacher and the students about the value of the experience.
- Share with a partner questions such as, What did you expect of the course? Did it live up to your expectations? What challenges were you faced with? This enable students to share their views privately with one other person.

- Discussion in groups and feedback later to the class. Why did you choose this course/workshop? What did you learn? What was easy/difficult?
- In groups, write brief responses on large sheets of paper to the following questions: What did you enjoy most? What did you like least? What did you learn that was new? If the course was to continue, what next? Display and discuss the results.

The information gained from these last two examples would be helpful for the organiser and teacher to take into account when planning future courses.

Complete an individual evaluation form. Questions could focus on such things as the teaching/learning experience; on the effectiveness of the process; information regarding the administration of the course.

Additional examples of evaluation forms are included in Chapter 4.

3

Composing, Performing, Appreciating

The 'dance as art' model is comprised of three strands: composing, performing and appreciating. As teachers of creative dance, we should be concerned that our students experience all three strands. They do not need to be evident in every class, or given equal attention, but students should have an understanding and appreciation of all the aspects.

Composing – to construct, form, arrange, put together, to make art work – is an essential element of all the arts. An important aspect of our work as teachers is to enable students to form their own dances – to compose, to choreograph. This process enables them to express ideas, thoughts and feelings, and communicate them through dance. It provides an opportunity for students to speak with their own voices in the production of a unique artistic statement.

Composing is the making of dances. The components of composing dance include:

- Imagining.
- Researching.
- Exploring.
- Improvising.
- Developing a dance vocabulary.
- Problem-solving.
- Decision-making.

- Selecting.
- Repeating.
- Refining.

From: Guidance on dance education in *Dance in Schools*, Arts Council of Great Britain, 1993.

The task of the teacher is to give opportunities for students to encounter all of these components. In order to achieve this, the teacher must know the students and know the subject. This will involve:

- By understanding the culture and interests of the students, setting appropriate and challenging tasks to allow them to explore different ideas to arrive at a finished product.
- Through knowledge of choreographic skills, structures and devices, being able to advise students to make appropriate choices about the order, selection and arrangement of the material.

It is particularly important for the choreographer to have a clear intention and understanding of what the dance composition is about. The task then is to find ways to express the meaning with clarity and integrity. This may not be clear at the beginning of the process. As choreographers we may not wish – or even be able – to verbalise every detail of our intention; but this should become evident as the work becomes defined. We should not baffle our audience (unless our intention is to baffle). All movement should be meaningful and be formed in a logical way – not a series of unrelated movements strung together, but an orderly arrangement, and a valid way to fulfil the intention.

The process of choreography is one of exploration and discovery. The teacher should guide each student to find ways to express his or her unique individuality. It is important to be aware of the difference between improvisation and structuring material. Forming material should not be encouraged until movement has been sufficiently explored. Students should be encouraged to find new ways to move and invent a variety of solutions to each task before making choices. They need to be challenged to extend their vocabulary and not fall back on familiar and comfortable movement patterns.

The teacher's role is not

Ludus Dance
Company summer
school, 1997.
Photo: Alan
Dowthwaite.

Creative class at
Rubicon Dance.
Photo: Peter Russell.

"to comfort the afflicted, but to afflict the comfortable."

R.M. Cohen (1991), *A Lifetime of Teaching*, Columbia University.

In this way our students grow and develop. Too much concern with structure too early on can become restrictive and produce boring, predictable movement. Equally important is knowing what you are *not* dealing with, and being selective about choices. The ability to analyse the work and to remove unnecessary, unrelated movement should be encouraged. The material should be allowed to shape the form rather than trying to fit it into a pre-determined structure. The logicality of the structure comes from the material itself.

As Blom and Chaplin suggest,

"Know what your intention is and say it with clarity and simplicity."

L. A. Blom & L. T. , Chaplin (1998), *The Intimate Act of Choreography*, Dance Books.

This is essential to the success of the task.

"Drawing out students' ideas, giving them the opportunity to put their ideas into movement, providing a secure atmosphere in which to do it, giving them courage to 'live dangerously', to dig into their own resources, monitoring and guiding them toward artistic clarity."

Dorothy Madden, in V. Preston-Dunlop (1995), *Dance Words*, Harwood Academic Publishers.

"The inventiveness of the human being is a constant surprise."

Dorothy Madden, in V. Preston-Dunlop (1995), *Dance Words*, Harwood Academic Publishers.

Composing

Talking with Choreographers

First I asked Erica Stanton, choreographer and teacher, her views on teaching choreography. She sees the process of choreography as one of constant change; of definition and redefinition, trial and error, with no hard-and-fast rules. She talked of the joy of participation in choreography workshops taught by gifted teachers who were provocative, stimulating, and sometimes highly critical. She became aware that in spite of their different approaches, there was some common ground. She indicated that these key features were:

- Staying true to themselves. Being clear in their point of view and not trying to be all things to all people.
- Making the crafting aspects exciting. Even space and time can be enticingly theatrical!
- Creating a trustful and fertile atmosphere, a place where people can make a mess and make mistakes.

She suggested that workshops dealing with composing should include some of the following:

- Thinking, imagining, moving (as a complex process of simultaneous decision-making).
- Improvisation (free and structured).
- Setting and learning new material.
- Performance of new material.
- Appraisal/feedback.

In discussing how teachers contribute to the process, she argued that there is no one ideal construct for the effective teaching of choreography, where we really wrestle with art and ideas. When a method of teaching emerges, whether in the form of a training programme or a handbook, for example, it won't necessarily work for all of us. So although it is very useful to have a few choreographers who are willing to share their ideas, that is only one way – and it is their way. It is important for a teachers to feel that their material is rooted in their own identities in order to feel natural and spontaneous.

Some questions to be considered:

- What are your dance skills?
- What are your skills in the other arts? Plunder them and exploit them.
- What are your preferences? Have a strong point of view so that your students can see it clearly and know what they are rebelling against when they are ready.
- Keep your observation skills acute. What are your students doing? How are they doing

it? Have they done it before? Are habits emerging? Is there a group choreographic identity?
- Know your own taste. Be particularly careful here. We can all get so enthralled by performance that we forget the look of the choreography.
- Try not to get into a routine. Move the goalposts and infuriate your students. But always keep your sense of humour.

Erica went on to express concern that in schools the identity of dance as an artistic endeavour can be lost in attempts to illuminate other areas of the curriculum. In such circumstances the teacher needs to answer the following questions:

- Is the dance material itself inventive?
- What do you see when you look at it?
- How do you feel when you look at it?
- How do you feel when you are doing it? These all-important sensual/kinaesthetic processes need time and the right kind of environment to bloom.

She said that, as teachers, we can all empower our students by teaching skills and offering them tools which enable them to make their own decisions about their choice of ideas, about the execution and presentation of those ideas, and about how they feel about their own and each other's dances. We are striving for an independence in the creative process which needs:

- Lots of workshops about how things work – body, space, time, dynamics, textures, and so on.
- Reinforcement of the relationship between dance and the other arts, in order to make composing a real cross-arts experience.
- Opportunities for playing and experimenting; finding out in a trustful but challenging environment.

Finally, Erica suggested that the most important thing for us to remember is that dance is art, and as such involves us in inspiration and aspiration. It rouses us and arouses us and is a great leveller. She quoted Iris Murdoch:

'Neurotransmission'
at Suffolk Dance.
Photo: Mike
Kwasniak.

"Art is very much to do with accident, with contingency, with detail, with self-expression, with trickery of all kinds, with magic."
Iris Murdoch (1978) in P. Conrady (1997) (ed.), *Existentialists and Mystics*, Chatto & Windus.

I also talked with Wayne McGregor and Rosemary Lee, two established choreographers, about their approach to their work because of the range and diversity of projects with which they have been involved. They have each choreographed works for various community groups as well as professional dancers.

I began by talking to Wayne McGregor. I had read a piece entitled 'Biteback' that he had written for *Animated* magazine, in response to Sue Akroyd's article, 'Whose Dance is it Anyway?' (Autumn 1996). Wayne spoke of how as a choreographer he has always tried to celebrate the individual. He stated: 'Whatever the context, the dancer and I have had equal ownership of the concept and ideas, their realisation, execution and articulation'.

I asked him the following questions:

- What is your process of choreography?
- How do the dancers affect the process?

He began by talking about how the dancers affect the process. He gave as an example a project for a group of boys who Chris Thomson (Director of the Education and Community Programme at Contemporary Dance Trust) had identified as having limited access to dance. The objective was to find a way to engage these young men in dance choreographically. What was to be required of them was a commitment, responsibility and an appreciation of the artistic imperative, with the performance as the goal.

Wayne described his method of work with them. During his first encounter with the group, he quickly got them engaged in movement. He was concerned to give them a kinetic sense of movement – not through a technical approach but by physical activities. He began with movements such as stretches and swings to give a rush of high energy and involve them quickly, without them thinking. He uses this approach with many of the groups he works with to introduce energetic, achievable challenges. He was concerned to introduce movement qualities which excite – travels, twists, turns, shifts across the space – motional aspects of movement. After twenty minutes of this kind of work the dancers should be hooked – as with this group of boys.

While this was happening Wayne would begin to assess the movement potential of each individual. How did they respond, join in, opt out? He might continue by introducing duets and would first spend some time developing partnering skills. For example, he might teach, in a didactic way, the skills necessary to complete a task such as pull, push, fall, fall, lift. He might then introduce a choreographic task and set out the structure. The vocabulary would be drawn from material already explored in the class.

Wayne often works in the same way with his company. As he knows his dancers very well, he might try to push them in unfamiliar ways. He draws on the strengths of individuals but wants to give new challenges rather than familiar ones which would not extend their movement vocabulary. The tasks might be more layered and the ideas developed more quickly than with an inexperienced group. Some days are more creative than others. He thinks it is important to be disciplined with time so that short-term goals can be achieved.

He gave an example of how he developed material for the choreography of his work *White Out*, a community project performed in 1998. He envisaged a neutral space where memory can vanish and return. He began by asking the boys to imagine a three-dimensional space such as a tunnel or a chasm. What is it like in this space? After improvising, they were asked to take three movements which gave a clear visual impression of the space – such as crawl, reach, pull away. They would then each have a movement sentence. He might encourage them to play around with the material before setting it. He might get them to build duets, for example: A performs his movement sentence while giving instructions to B, such as touch my arm, pull me up, hold my head, and so on.

Wayne intervenes when necessary, to clarify the movement and to add new challenges. He does not like to form work too quickly but prefers to give time to develop and manipulate movement material to see what emerges. Sometimes a session on content might be followed by one on structure.

He talks with the dancers about what he sees, the special moments, how to achieve the particular quality required. This encourages them to work with the material and not to be too easily satisfied; but he does give time limits, to keep everyone on task.

As a choreographer, he has questions to ask. He is interested in the place that dance can explore: the technical, visual dominated world we live in. The dancers help him towards answers. He is aware of generational differences and sees that the response of young people shapes the work in a particular way. He wants to give opportunities to allow each individual to express him or herself. He is concerned to give all of his dancers equal worth and to value each one's unique contribution. As he states in his article:

"The art of making dances involves a unique dialogue, a dialogue which constantly develops and changes as individuals participate."
Wayne McGregor (1996), 'Biteback', *Animated*, Autumn.

Talking with choreographer, Rosemary Lee, I asked her the same questions:

- What is your process of choreography?
- How do the dancers affect the process?

She suggested that it might be easier to describe the working process of specific pieces, as it can vary, rather than to talk of her work in general. We began with her most recent work – *greenman* (1998)– a film commissioned by BBC2 and the Arts Council of England for the 'Dance for the Camera' series, with dancer Simon Whitehead.

Working with film gives Rosemary the opportunity to confront issues of narrative and linear form, but this was not of primary concern at the beginning of this project. She had a strong sense of what the work would be about and its location – for *greenman*, a mediaeval-looking tower (in fact, a folly) and its surrounding landscape. It was to be a solo for a man (she is curious about solo work and is interested in exploring the one-to-one relationship of choreographer and dancer as a contrast to the large community groups she has worked with). In *greenman* and with other solo pieces, she is concerned to bring out the potential in the chosen dancer (she normally does not audition for dancers, but invites people to dance for her). As well as Simon's obvious movement qualities, she was interested to explore those less apparent – eccentricity, vulnerability, fragility.

She wanted the movement to be awkward, uncomfortable. A desk was used in the piece, which came to represent a sense a sense of safety and security for the dancer – his home – and also made the connection to the outside world. Both the site itself and the process of moving inside and outside, would make specific demands on the movement material.

The first rehearsal was spent finding ways to physicalise the character. For example, a task was set to link two body parts – the sternum and the back of the knees – in conversation, pulling together or apart. Through movement tasks like this, the character began to develop. She knew she wanted some animal-like movement material, and a coat was used to explore movement possibilities: to cover up, emerge from, be a hard shell. As rehearsals progressed, different dramatic scenarios were suggested involving the desk: move with the desk, lie on it, think of it as an altar, as a piano, as your refuge. A lot of time was spent outside at the sites exploring actions, such as walking, skipping, scattering, jumping.

Selection were made as things emerged. Rosemary uses a notebook to record ideas and video to review material, which was helpful for this piece. However she has some doubts about using video for work in theatre as it does not truly represent what is seen.

The second piece we discussed was *The Galliard – Every Move before Breakfast* (1994), with dancer Gill Clarke. The original idea was based on the image of a queen – Elizabeth, or the Red Queen from *Alice in Wonderland*. Court dance was to influence the use of space, which used squares, circles, diagonals. The movement was to have a relentless driving quality (the image of dancing continuously from *The Red Shoes*). The dancer was particularly important to the work. Rosemary wanted to make a piece for Gill that would bring out her wonderful performing quality and the way in which she connects movement so seamlessly, always finding a flow – an inner logic, a fluid pathway through her body – but would also include very different dynamics of anger and attack, cutting the pathway of the flow.

She wanted Gill to be able to use all her technical skills and imbue them with the character. In rehearsal, she set various improvisation tasks with images to influence the quality of the movement – images such as passionate Morris dancer, a knife-edge, scissors. Lame, dragging movements were explored to de-beautify the material.

An example of development was as follows: Gill was asked to create a phrase using a series of four arcs, made with the head, hip, hand and ankle. This was developed by travelling the phrase on an arc. The next stage was to fit the phrase to the melody line of some music.

A lot of movement material was generated and the task then was how to unravel it. Time was spent improvising with the movement phrases to help decide on the structuring. This is the most difficult task. The context got richer as the movement, which felt like a mad queen, developed.

Rosemary was also invited to make a work for the Lilian Baylis Over 60s Performance Group. She knew the group and wanted to develop a work inspired by the people – their experience and presence, their ability to speak their own minds. She wanted to present who they were individually as well as collectively and to give them a kind of choreographic challenge different from what they had had previously. The work *5 Songs* (1996) was to be about loss and letting go – both themes with which they were familiar.

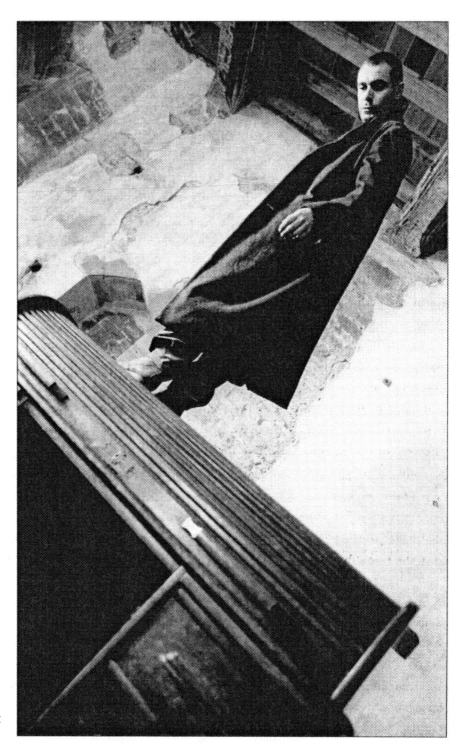

Simon Whitehead
in Rosemary Lee's
greenman.
Photo: © Margaret
Williams

The music – set to five traditional British songs sung by Kathleen Ferrier – was very important to the work. The dancers were familiar with her singing. Her heartfelt simplicity, the rawness and truthfulness of her singing, made a link with the women and their histories. Rosemary wanted to use these qualities in the movement – to pare down what the dancers could offer to find their own inner calm, grace and presence.

She divided them into two groups of ten dancers so that they could be seen better as individuals in two songs. She worked on simple concepts, such as a wall of people slowly advancing toward the audience. She used the images of a huge headdress, and a gown with a train of memories, to influence the quality of a simple walk. Some gestures were included – catching heavy rain drops in upturned palms; catching them randomly. This unpredictability changed the focus of the audience to different individuals. Another gestural idea was that of touching one's cheek, and touching an imaginary cheek.

To achieve the quality of grace and inner calm she wanted, she introduced a task which was to move through the space, first disturbing the air and then to show the contrast of moving without disturbing it.

She also introduced an idea which she had previously used in *Egg Dances* (1988), a movement which began with exposing the palms of the hand and rising on the tip toe. The other dancers came close to give support. The supporting became physical – touching, holding, and the same movement was repeated followed by falling.

From our conversation, it became apparent that Rosemary's method of work does not radically change. In all the work we discussed, she starts with the intention of the piece. In each case, she is very much influenced by what the dancers bring of themselves – their skill, experience, background. She is keen to use these qualities but also to take the dancers somewhere new. She knows the qualities, mood, intention and atmosphere that she wants. She doesn't make movement and give it to the dancer, but, through improvisation, finds ways to give her intention substance and form embodied in the dancer.

Note: Another description of working with the Lilian Baylis Over 60s Performance Group by Suz Broughton is included in the following section of the book.

Performing

Each art form allows us to express ourselves in a unique way and the experience of one art form is not interchangeable and cannot be substituted for another. For an art form to be valued, it needs to be perceived. Dance is the least visible of the arts. It is transitory, in that it is of the moment. Once it happens, it is over. The ephemeral nature of dance means that, although it may remain in the memory, it leaves behind no visible traces.

If we compare dance with music, the visual arts and drama, dance is much less obvious in our environment. We can hear music constantly on radio, tapes, CDs, in lifts, shops, concert halls, stadiums. Examples of the visual arts are all around us in magazines, posters, advertisements, books, galleries, museums. It is possible to see drama each day on our television screens as well as in cinemas and theatres. Dance is much less in evidence.

The venues for dance are few and far between, and opportunities to see dance performances are restricted. We need to encourage audiences for dance. For people to have a better understanding and appreciation of dance and to raise the profile of dance, it has to be seen in performance as well as experienced by the dancer.

Although our dance classes might be mostly concerned with *process* – that is with the activity of dancing, the development of physical skills, or dance-making and composing dances – there may be occasions when it is important to bring the work to culmination and to give attention to the *product* in performance. Performance opportunities can be considered at a number of different levels. They may be informal, a sharing of work with others, an in-house event or a more formal demonstration or presentation of work. Working towards a performance has an entirely different focus to that of the dance class. In the dance class the work is ongoing and involves a process of revisiting; that is to say, it is formative and dynamic – concerned with focusing upon that moment in time. For a performance, however, there is a sense of building to the event, of the summative happening, a conclusion, and then an opportunity to move on. In performance, dancers have the occasion to combine all the knowledge and skills gained in the dance class and embody them in their performance. It is important to recognise the value of the process leading towards it. Working for a performance, dancers have the opportunity, through practice and repetition, to refine their work and develop accuracy and fluency in their movement. The rehearsal period enables attention to be given to developing their expressive and interpretive skills.

As well as the activity of dancing, a good dance class would always involve some aspect of appreciation – which could be as simple as considering some questions about the activity posed by the teacher. At a more sophisticated level, students might be asked to examine a work critically. In both of these cases, performing is about the activity of dancing. However, performing can be a much more formal occasion where an audience is invited to view, and sometimes to pay to see a dance performance. This gives a different focus and intention to a piece which may have previously only been observed by members of the group.

Is it important to offer performing opportunities to our students? I think it is – if it is appropriate for the members of the group. It is not always so for every group, and indeed performance for some groups – because of their nature and expectations – would be unacceptable. People who would not wish to perform should not be forced to do so.

Even some performance groups might include individuals who may need some gentle persuasion to convince them to take that first exhilarating step. Apart from building confidence, the thrill, excitement and satisfaction felt after achieving a successful performance is hard to beat.

What follows are some general principles that are relevant to all groups, regardless of age or composition. The same conceptual unities apply whatever the context. The response will be more or less sophisticated depending upon the age, experience and ability of the group. However, the demand for high expectations and professionalism should apply, whatever the group.

The Rehearsal Process

This gives the dancers the opportunity, through practising and refining the work, to develop accuracy and fluency in their performance. Dancers require time to become familiar with musical accompaniment. Knowing music, through dancing to it, is a different experience from that of simply listening. The response should not be a mechanical one, concerned only with counts, but should involve the ability to recall and appreciate the phrasing, anticipate the changes of rhythm, and respond to the troughs and swells of dynamics in the body. Sensitivity to the accompaniment, to the use of space and to other performers should be encouraged as the rehearsal period progresses. Dancers need to have a clear understanding of the intention of the work. They need to work at a deep level to improve the quality of the movement and to develop their own artistic interpretation.

The preparation immediately prior to the event should be thorough. It is important to

Photo: Adam
Eastland. Contem-
porary Dance Trust.

warm the body and alert and concentrate the mind. Just before the performance begins, calmness should be encouraged by suggesting each individual runs through the dance in their minds.

Performance Skills

The better the advance preparation, the more students understand what is required of them, and the more likely the success of the venture. Students need to be aware of the seriousness of the enterprise and be fully committed to it. Work should be well rehearsed for the students to be secure in the movement. For this to happen, they must have owner-ship of the movement and not be embarrassed or uncomfortable. They need to understand the movement and its intention and not be dependent on the teacher, or have to copy someone else.

Emphasis should be given to filling the movement, whether the movement is initiated from the centre of the body or peripherally. Dancers need to be aware of the importance of beginnings and endings. Beginning is not simply being still – it is about being alert, prepared mentally and physically for what is to follow, focused. Ending is not just a stop – it is about holding on to the clarity of the movement, complete stillness, nothing moving, holding the gaze, conclusion. Transitions should be well rehearsed so that there is no stop in the flow of the movement, and the work appears to be seamless.

Good use of focus is a way of giving definition to a dance. Where and how a dancer looks, gazes, and with what depth and intensity, can give clarity to the work. This can highlight moments of stillness; it can be used to emphasise a movement through space, either simultaneously or leading, following, opposing a movement. Strong use of focus which extends out through the space can draw the audience to the dancer. Focus is an important ingredient in a number of different dance styles, including South Asian dance, and Spanish dance.

When performing, there should be no loss of concentration:

- No coming out of the movement.
- No fidgeting with clothes or hair.
- No whispering nor talking to each other.

Bill Cratty in rehearsal with Transitions Dance Company, Laban Centre London. Photo: Chris Nash.

– unless the choreography includes any of these things, in which case they should be performed with clarity of intention.

Before work is performed, the dancers need to understand the intention, style and form of the piece. They need to have an appreciation of the choreographer's vision and purpose and of any distinctive characteristics of the work, as well as a clear understanding of its structure. They should be familiar with the requirements in terms of the performance space, entrances and exits, lighting and special effects. These can often be a problem, as time in the performance space can be costly and limited. It is helpful if the rehearsal space is set up to simulate the requirement of where the work is eventually to be performed. Students need time to become familiar and comfortable with costumes or props if they are to be used. Neither should get in the way of the movement.

- Try to foster sensitivity to each other among the dancers.
- Encourage them to think of themselves as members of a company, with each person being important to the communal success of the venture. Everyone needs to feel they have a valuable contribution to make.

The essence of good performing skills is the way in which the idea – the mental image – is given objective reality. Three essential ingredients for success are the effective use of:

- Interpretation.
- Projection.
- Artistry.

It is difficult to define any one of them independently of the others. They are inextricably linked and, in addition, successful performance involves a mixture of all three. Beginners in dance might well only touch upon some of these aspects; with experience, the greater level of understanding enables a deeper and more sensitive use of them. For the audience to value a performance it should have integrity and this should be reflected in the commitment and professionalism of the dancers. This is the case whatever their age or experience.

Interpretation:

To interpret is:

> "To make the dance come to life."
> Bonnie Bird in V. Preston-Dunlop (1995), *Dance Words*, Harwood Academic Publishers.

A knowledge and understanding of the choreographer's style is necessary for a dancer to interpret a choreographer's work effectively. By paying close attention to the choreographer's intention, the dancer can illuminate rather than disguise the meaning of the dance. Interpretation is a kind of translation. An interpretation is unique in that no two people will interpret a dance in the same way. Each individual will bring something different and special to the work every time it is performed.

> "Dancers give the dance shades of character, quality and meaning which are not necessarily prescribed by the choreographer."
> Pauline Hodgens, in J. Adshead (1988), *Dance Analysis*, Dance Books.

Projection:

Projection is concerned with the relationship between the dancer and the viewer. It is about giving the choreographer's intention visible energy, which is perceived in the dancer's body. Choreographers have differing views about how they wish to communicate their work.

'Street Beat' at Suffolk Dance, 1998. Photo: Mike Kwasniak.

Locus, choreographed by Erica Stanton and Marion Gough. Photo: Tony Nandi.

Some postmodern choreographers are concerned with *containment* and the internalising of movement – about implosion. They do not wish to go out of themselves into another's feelings, but rather to focus upon an inner intention. This can result in the focus being contained and the work becoming exclusive. This demands a different kind of attention from the audience.

I see successful projection as a generous, constructive relationship between the choreographer, the dancer and the audience. The dancer gives definition to the intention and quality of the work, which is recognised by the audience. This kind of projection requires dancers to fill the movement and extend it beyond themselves – to 'reach out' metaphorically and encourage the viewer to participate.

"Projection involves throwing the energy out from the body so as to give a quality of life to the movement."
Linda Rickett-Young (1996), *Essential Guide to Dance,* Hodder & Stoughton.

Artistry:

Artistry is concerned with more than merely the physicality of the body and technical skill.

We use the term 'artistry' when the mind, body and spirit of the dancer combine to transfigure the movement and make it different and special. Through artistry we are made aware of the process of transforming the ordinary into the extraordinary. Artistry brings out the significance of the work and enables us to perceive the dancer and the dance in a new way.

Why Perform? Something from the Field

I talked with two colleagues concerned with performance about their work with two very different groups – Avril Hitman, freelance teacher, founder, and artistic director of Magpie Dance, and Suz Broughton, dancer teacher and choreographer about her work with the Lilian Baylis Over 60s Performing Group.

I asked them each to describe the nature of the group and then to answer the following questions:

- Why do you think it is important for the group to perform?
- What do they gain from the experience?
- How do you see your role in helping them to achieve a successful outcome?

First, Avril Hitman's response regarding Magpie Dance.

Magpie Dance, based in Bromley, is a company of ten adults – five men and five women – with learning disabilities. It aims to enrich the lives of disadvantaged people through dance and the performing arts. Magpie enables people with learning disabilities to take a full and integrated part in the artistic life of the community and so increase awareness of the achievements and potential of people with learning disabilities.

The group grew out of weekly dance sessions, when it became very clear that they were of great benefit to the members in developing dance skills, gaining tremendous confidence, increasing concentration and self-esteem. Magpie Dance now undertakes community, education and performance work. Performance offers the opportunities to expand and develop the skills of the Magpie dancers by working with professional dance artists and musicians.

Magpie's first public performance was in 1993 at the South Bank Centre, London – a collaboration with choreographer Jasmine Pasch, musician Ian Stewart and writer-in-residence John Agard to create a dance piece, which led to a performance at the Ballroom Blitz Festival with didgeridoo player Richard Walley. Many thousands of people have seen Magpie perform in different venues since 1994. These have included performances at venues such as the Royal Albert Hall at the sixtieth anniversary celebrations of the Central Council For Physical Recreation, Magpie being the only disability group performing.

Avril discussed the following questions with a couple of volunteer workers and they came up with these responses.

Why is it important for the group to perform?

Working for a common goal. The dancers are viewed from another perspective by family and carers. A concern for the dance company as a whole to succeed. A sense of self-worth. Performance shows those with learning difficulties in a positive light. It is an opportunity for them to take a part in the artistic life of the community through performance. A chance to say, 'I can do it.'

What do they gain from the experience?

Self-esteem, confidence, personal skills, and so on. The discipline of rehearsal is important, as people respect being challenged both mentally and physically. The dancers are taking responsibility not only for themselves, but as a company. The learning ability of the dancers gets better due to past experience. There is the opportunity to build on different choreographic experience and working in different musical styles which help the development of the skills of the dancers. (Magpie has worked in a variety of styles, including jazz and contemporary. One example of a new style for the dancers was that of street performance, which was sponsored by Marks and Spencer. This took place on two occasions, the most recent being in Bromley High Street as part of Bromley Arts Festival (1998.)

Most of the dancers do not find it easy to express their feelings and ideas in words; but some of their personal comments follow:

Linda said it 'makes me feel happy.' She has a sense of showing others what you can achieve. Linda feels that she has changed since joining Magpie, which 'makes me feel like an adult'.

Magpie Dance Company. Photo: Phil Polglaze.

After the performance at Cardiff in front of 1000 people, Linda said 'I did it!' She feels 'wonderful' when she's on stage in the spotlight.

Hugh said, 'It's exciting to perform – very tasteful'. He does feel nervous before performing but once he starts dancing he loses the feeling of nervousness. Hugh doesn't mind going over and over something to get it right as he feels it's important to get the right moves.

John enjoys the audience watching him perform. It has become easier to be a Magpie dancer. 'The bow at the end makes me feel good. I like being in the spotlight on stage.'

Andrew wanted to join Magpie. 'I like the people clapping and watching. It makes me feel very good.'

David said, 'The bigger the audience, the better!' He doesn't get nervous and feels good after a performance.

Sue said, 'I don't know, I just love it!' Standing in the wings during one performance she said, 'I love this dancing!'

How do you see your role in helping them to achieve a successful outcome?

Avril replied:

The volunteers felt that I am able to use my past experience as a teacher to bring out the best in people. I am able to see the potential of the company. Who is able to do what; helping to bring out each individual's ability. Helping the dancers to realise their full potential. I have some knowledge of what other professional artists Magpie can work with, for example collaborations with other dancers, musicians, different art forms.

It is important that there is co-ordination with the families and carers about the dancers' activities. They need to support Magpie practically, for example by seeing that the right costumes are taken to the right place at the right time, providing money for the day. I arrange transport as necessary such as hire of the minibus and drivers and make sure that there is the right amount of able-bodied support for each project.

Next, Suz Broughton talking about The Lilian Baylis Over 60s Performing Group.

The group arose out of the Over 60s club established in 1989. It was set up by Carolyn Naish, who recognised there was a need to make the arts more accessible to the older generation. She organised workshops and demonstrations held by a variety of professional companies in a range of styles, and scheduled performances at convenient times and at affordable prices. She was intent on providing a place which gave older people an active role in the arts and allowed them to explore their own creative energy, which for many of them had been denied an outlet over the years due to work and family responsibilities.

"If I could live my life all over again, I'd go on stage, And I wouldn't let any body stop me!"

Jean Morgan, in *Shall We Dance?* (Carlton TV, 1995, a documentary on the Lilian Baylis group)

In 1990, after giving a workshop attended by the Queen, some of the members expressed a desire to perform. The performing group was established in 1991, and was initially made up of 24 women aged from 62 to 84 years. In general, they work with a new choreographer each term and these have included Royston Maldoom, Rosemary Lee, Mark Baldwin, Sarah Rubidge, Emily Burns and Fergus Early. They have performed in a wide variety of theatres and have gone from strength to strength, gaining confidence and demanding new challenges. The performing group still has around 24 members, until recently all women. The oldest is now in her eighty-sixth year.

Why do you think it is important that they perform?

Suz responded that the sheer enjoyment and excitement that is gained from being on stage is the most important reason why members of this group continue to do work towards performances:

> "I dance for the love of it. Performance work spreads joy and dance in itself is joyful to do, even when it is difficult."
> Pat Hursey, 1997

> "Inside I feel all churned up and lovely and happy and then when you've done it and you've done it well, you think – oh that was good, that went well and you've got that feeling of well- being. It's a wonderful feeling. You kind of want to tell everybody I was in that, in case you didn't recognise me, I was in that."
> Ann Ebbs, in *Shall We Dance?*

The first time they walked out on to the stage to perform, there was a lot of trepidation and anxiety amongst them. One of their main fears was that they would be ridiculed by younger people, and especially dancers. It is commonplace to see youth groups and lithe, supple bodies in dance companies, but the opportunities for this same level of expression and performance for the older age range, especially senior citizens, is very much neglected. Many of the group hadn't danced since their schooldays, forty or fifty years ago, and one of them was dancing for the first time at the age of 81. Clearly, these people were facing more challenges than the average dance group!

However, the immense appreciation and applause shown by the audience at the end of

Lilian Baylis Over 60s Performance Group. Photo: Vanessa Winship.

their first piece confirmed to the dancers that they had the power and the ability to command the stage as well as any other performers.

Having gone through the experience of success together, it served to bond the group, and their confidence grew both on an individual level and in the company as a whole.

> "I was actually shopping – when someone came up to me and said 'Excuse me, have I seen you dance?' and I thought, I've made it! I've made it in Sainsbury's."
> Sandie Barwick, from documentary footage by Sally Webb

They began trusting what they were capable of achieving together and realised that they had as much right as any other performing company to be taken seriously.

> "In a team, cooperation is all important – togetherness must be achieved and determination to hold one's audience."
> Jeanette White, 1997

"Performing gives me a great sense of excitement . . . When I get out on the stage I forget the nerves and the adrenaline flows and I don't want the performance to be over. I really love it!"
Ann Ebbs, in *Shall We Dance?*

"The importance of stage dance is that it brings the work you do to the attention of others, which encourages them in turn."
Pat Hursey, 1997

This last comment highlights another important reason for such a group to be performing to public audiences: as many people as possible can see the type of work that can be accomplished by older dancers. It is a generally held assumption, by both younger and older people alike, that the older you get, the more invisible you become. Such assumptions make the work of this group even more valuable and raises the profile of this age group.

The work also provides an opportunity for friends and relations to see the dancers in a very different light from how they are usually perceived within the family network.

The very presence of these dancers on stage brings into question the notion of beauty in dance. The group have reduced their audience to tears by the sheer power of their performance, performances which blow open the definitions of aesthetics and beauty of the body and its movement. As one of the members said:

"I always dreamed of becoming a dancer. I never dreamed that at my age I'd be doing things like this, I thought I'd be sitting at home with the knitting."
Ann Ebbs, in *Shall We Dance?*

While such activities as knitting and similar hobbies suit some people, they obviously do not suit everyone; and yet there remains very limited access for the older person to pursue a wider range of interests. It is therefore important to be constantly challenging such stereotyping, and both to remind the older person of what they can achieve and to question any preconceptions and limited expectations of older people by those who are younger.

The importance of performing for this group is therefore twofold. It gives a sense of value and well-being to each one of them and it opens up the opportunity for others to see the extraordinary work that can be accomplished by older people. This physically active image of the older person presents a positive model for growing old and explodes the myths of what can be achieved by this age group.

What do they gain from it?

Suz replied that performing gives this group a place in the dance world, where before they were only spectators. At the beginning of their first meetings, they were given demonstrations and lectures about events taking place in the theatres, but very little of this was providing them with any representations of their own generation. Now they are the ones to be providing this for others and that gives them a sense of pride and pleasure.

The members of the group joined for many different reasons. Some had an interest in the theatre, others wanted to meet new people. Rose Teague, the oldest member of the group, joined when her husband passed away a few years ago. As she says,

> "It keeps you young. I looked after my husband for years [and when he died] I came here and it has given me a new lease of life."
> Rose Teague, *Saga Magazine* 1993, article by Paul Lewis.

From joining for all these different reasons, many of them then found themselves, a few months later,

> "doing something that I never expected I would ever do… to dance on stage."
> Gladys Hillman, from documentary footage by Sally Webb

Gladys Hillman only joined because her only local club was a bingo club and she wasn't interested in that. She had no initial intention of becoming a dancer, but has now been performing for five years and, as she says herself,

> "It's great fun and I wouldn't miss it for the world."
> Gladys Hillman, from documentary footage by Sally Webb

This story is the same for many of them. From that very first rehearsal, they have now gained an extraordinary sense of achievement. Many of them never imagined that, at their age, they would be capable of taking such a stance in the dance world and of being able to learn a whole new language, exploring and developing their creativity within this medium.

"It's marvellous to be a dancer – (it is) beyond my wildest dreams."
Ann Ebbs, in *Shall We Dance?*

The group provides a strong sense of belonging for the members, as they become involved in the whole process that performance work encompasses, including costuming, technical and dress rehearsals. From early on, many of the members had an understanding of all this from the workshops and demonstrations given by visiting companies to the Club. It is now their turn to be on the receiving end of all this work, and, as Heather Elkin said,

"Being in costume under the lights is a wonderful feeling."
Heather Elkin, 1997

Sharing a laugh, learning new skills together and the social side of rehearsals are important parts of the whole process. The performing element strengthens the feelings between them as they all go through, experiencing the nerves and taking the risk that live performance brings, and, of course, enjoying the outcome together.

Having been involved with this group from their first performances, it was wonderful for Suz to see just how much they have developed their confidence, both on the level of the performer and also on the more personal level. The knowledge that they can achieve such things together so successfully in one area feeds through to other areas of their lives and gives them an empowering sense of their abilities.

How do you see your role in helping them to achieve a successful outcome?

Suz responded:

I have created three pieces for this group, and each time I work with them I have three aims. First, I try to ensure that each rehearsal is as enjoyable as is possible for everyone. Second, I present them with a challenge. As the performance approaches, the third aim is to make them feel as confident as possible with the work. At this later stage, extra time is sometimes needed to just sit and listen to the music, clarifying counts and phrasing. For each piece their needs vary, and the dancers dictate the nature of these last rehearsals depending on their requirements.

The rehearsals start with a half-hour warm up, which incorporates a range of exercises. Some familiar movements for the joints and spine will be done first. These will be repeated week after week to ensure that everyone knows exactly what they are doing and no injuries are caused by starting the session with unknown movements. This is followed by faster exercises with changes of directions or counts to awaken the body and mind. Finally, some movements from the piece will be included in an exercise, partly to start focusing the mind on the particular quality of the work, and partly to practise any difficult movements.

The next hour-and-a-half is spent working on the choreography. Fortunately I was familiar with this group before I began choreographing with them, so I was aware of their capabilities. I plan each session beforehand, so that when we work there are clear intentions for the dancers. This leaves them free to work on the movement material and quality. Within this planning, though, it is necessary to adapt in case any problems arise. This is especially important with the more challenging moves such as floor or lifting work.

With this group, there are only a few who are unable to go down to the floor.

"If you put me on the floor, you'll have to come and pick me up again!"
Vi Adams, in *Shall We Dance?*

In the piece *Even Ground* (1994), I choreographed their floor work in couples with one of them remaining standing. This left them free to chose who felt easiest about which part to dance and embraced everyone's capabilities.

The quality of movement in this piece was slow and sustained, with the dancers working on the idea of calling and beckoning to each other. For their next piece – *Rodeo*, danced to Aaron Copland's music – they had requested that they work on a faster piece, a contrast to many of their previous dances. My role with this work was to rise to the challenge that they had set for me as well as ensure that the faster movement didn't exclude any of the dancers who were more unsteady on their feet. The speed of the piece was therefore portrayed by some fast footwork, but it mostly relied on brisk, gestural movements of the hands and changes of direction with the body. Shifting of the space between groups of dancers gave the audience a strong sense of pace, without pushing the dancers too fast. Precise timing and specific use of body language was demanded in order to clearly establish the atmosphere and intention of the whole piece.

In both of these pieces, the dancers were given time for their own creative input. For the first few rehearsals, we discussed the ideas behind the pieces and worked on an initial phrase of movement. From there, they were able to explore and create their own movements while staying true to the integrity of the ideas. They were also able to work with a greater understanding of the particular style of the movement vocabulary. This encouraged them to move away from habitual movement patterns and thereby broaden their range of creativity.

The existence of this performing group continues to expand and deepen the understanding, for its members and audiences alike, of the importance of this kind of work. There is no limit to the imagination of the human spirit, and this group strives to show that age is no obstacle to the enjoyment that the freedom of movement and creativity can bring.

"I have only lived in the last twenty years and there is no end to the lovely things you can do; there really isn't."
Jean Morgan, in *Shall We Dance?*

Appreciating .

An essential part of good dance teaching, as well as working towards improving performing and composing skills, is to raise awareness and deepen understanding of aspects of appreciation. The ability to perceive, recognise, interpret and discriminate, contributes to making dance an intense experience.

As teachers, we need to lead our students towards:

"the development of interpretive and discriminative skills, together with the specialist knowledge in respect of works of art and forms of expression."
R.W. Witkin, 'The Concept of Development in Aesthetic Education', in M. Ross *The Development of Aesthetic Experience*, Pergamon Press.

Appreciation includes:

- The dance critic reviewing a professional dance performance.
- A choreographer discussing his/her work.
- Children looking at and talking about each others' work.
- An audience's response to a work

During a discussion with dance artist Madalena Victorino, she suggested that appreciation has two dimensions: one of a cognitive nature, where one may develop a way of analysing, describing and perhaps even deconstructing the work under observation; the other affective in nature, where one may feel, sense, perceive in a more intuitive and subjective way. Appreciation, then, involves reason and feeling, imagination and reality. Madalena believes the arts are concerned with creating narratives about a certain interpretation of the world. This necessarily involves a subjective (emotions, sensations, feelings, memories) and an objective (concepts, language, form, structure) approach towards its making, and it is the blending of such aspects that make the arts such an important element of human existence and of education itself.

A synthesis of both the subjective and objective responses helps us to find meaning in dance. These responses become more acute as we gain experience as interpreters and become more accomplished in analysing dance.

Susan Leigh Foster argues that:

"Only the viewer who retains visual, aural and kinaesthetic impressions of the dance as it unfolds in time can compare succeeding moments of the dance, noticing similarities, variations, and contrasts and comprehending large patterns – phrases of movement and sections of the dance and finally the dance as a whole."

Susan Leigh Foster (1986), *Reading Dance*, University of California Press.

This implies that we need to acquire knowledge, skills, experience, to be able to 'read' and understand dance.

"The aim of criticism in the arts is, in the broad sense of these terms, to *understand* or to grasp the *meanings* of the work of art. That is to say – the aim of criticism is understanding."

Graham McFee (1992), *Understanding Dance*, Routledge.

Madalena Victorino spoke of the importance of developing a sense of appreciation with students as soon as possible. It is an essential element of their personal development in dance. If successful, it can give a perspective which is informed, generous and sensitive.

How are we to go about helping our students to gain this understanding? To be able to perceive, translate, make sense of dance? To use informed judgements? Are there systems which can help this process?

One possible example is Liz Lerman's 'critical response process'. Lerman points out that much criticism tells you more about the interpreter's biases and expectations than about the piece in question. ('What I criticised in the work was that it wasn't like mine'.) The 'critical response process' provides the creator and observers with a supportive environment for dialogue. The process consists of six steps:

Wayne McGregor at the 'Neurotransmission' project at Suffolk Dance. Photo: Mike Kwasniak.

- Step One: Affirmation.
  Affirmative responses from the observers.
- Step Two: Artist as questioner.
  The creator asks the observers specific questions.
- Step Three: Responders ask the questions.
  They form their opinions into neutral – that is, non-judgemental – questions.
- Step Four: Opinion time.
  Responders ask permission to state an opinion.
- Step Five: Subject matter discussion.
  Discussion about the content of the work.
- Step Six: Working on the work.
  The artist may wish to continue work on a particular section.

L. Lerman (1993), 'Critical Response in the Field', *High Performance*, Winter.

I have participated in workshops – in the UK and in the US – where this process was used. The structure for the responses is very clear and, in all cases I experienced, provided a supportive, affirmative environment for the choreographer – but a somewhat restrictive one for the observer. As with any process, participants need to become familiar and trained in the method for it to work effectively. For me, however, it lacks the immediacy of being able to respond in a critical way and deal with the work in a rigorous, challenging manner. It may be that, in the American context, colleagues are more in tune with the Lerman approach.

Making and engaging in art *is* subjective. It is about giving form to feelings, emotions, sensations and memories – and the response that this evokes. The way we view a dance work is coloured by our personal histories, our socio-cultural backgrounds, our likes and dislikes. Even so, although appreciation of dance is inherently subjective, it need not be capricious. We need to move towards a structure for appreciation which can be supportive to the creator but still has rigour and challenge. We can use clear criteria based upon recognised knowledge, skills and experience.

One set of suggestions comes from the Arts Council document *Dance in Schools* (1993):

"Dance can be appreciated through performing and composing. The components of appreciating dance include:

observing

responding

describing

recognising

reflecting

discerning

interpreting

comparing and contrasting

analysing

decision making

making judgments

evaluating

developing a critical language."

Arts Council (1993), *Dance in Schools*

As teachers, we should be giving our students opportunities to experience all these components. In the section on 'Lesson Structure' in *In Touch With Dance* (Gough 1993), appreciation and evaluation were placed at the end of the lesson when work might be performed, viewed and discussed. This may have implied that they only occur at this time, but of course this should not be the case. Both students and teachers should be continually evaluating and reflecting on their progress and effectiveness. Evaluating is covered at some length in other parts of this book.

Appreciation, particularly, should not be seen as an activity which only occurs at the conclusion of a class. We should be trying to develop the appreciation skills of our students throughout the work. Just as, in performing and choreographing, the level and complexity of the task varies with the knowledge, skill and understanding of the students, so too with appreciation. The teacher needs to offer increasingly complex experiences which challenge students to consider, discuss and justify their opinions. This enhances their ability to analyse critically and have a deeper appreciation of their own work and that of others.

What follows are a number of examples of ways in which we can begin to heighten and extend students' appreciation skills when observing dance works. This is developed from a section in *In Touch with Dance* (Gough 1993):

- Watch, recall and describe. (What did you see?)
- What do you think the dance is about? How does it make you feel?
- How is the dance put together? (Structure and content).
- In what ways does it remind you of other dance works? (Compare and contrast).
- Make a critical analysis of the dance (Which part has most significance? Is any part confusing? Is anything missing? What should happen next?).

Working towards increasing this understanding may be achieved in a number of ways during the process of a class/workshop:

- Generally, involving everyone.
- Showing an individual example.
- Observing and responding to a partner's work.
- A more formal showing and evaluation of work.

This may be done by the teacher simply posing questions while the students are working. These may or may not require verbal answers. Such questions also help to engage students in the activity, for example:

- What happens when . . . ?
- How has the quality of the movement changed?

Another way is for students to show their work to a partner. Ask them:

- Discuss what you see.
- What did you find to be particularly interesting?

After a more formal showing and viewing of students' work, ask questions which all of the class can respond to:

- How did X solve the problem?
- How are Y and Z's solutions to the task different?

Just as students need to be trained in performance skills so that they become aware of the

Rubicon Dance, integrated deaf and disabled workshop, Romania. Photo: Eric Hands.

preparation, concentration and commitment involved, so the observer needs to understand what s/he needs to bring to the activity: respect and sensitivity for the creator and the performer(s), attention to the observation, willingness to talk about what they see.

It is helpful to give observation guidelines to an inexperienced group about what they might look for. Not just 'What did you like?', but, for example:

- How was the space used?
- Describe how the dance began and ended.
- What should happen next?

Some teachers have the idea that this kind of approach can only be achieved with teenagers and adults. This need not be so. Young children, when well trained, have the ability to describe and discuss what they see most competently. I was delighted to encounter the sophisticated level of understanding with which a group of seven and eight-year-olds at Lucas Vale School, south-east London, were able to compare and contrast their work with that, on videotape, of a professional dance company. The discussion was expertly led by their teacher, Jenny Hill.

Most of our students will not end up being dancers and may not continue to perform or choreograph, but they will retain an understanding and appreciation of the art form.

4

Promoting Good Practice

Teaching Skills for Dancers

Increasingly over the past few years I have been invited to take courses for such groups as:

- Professional dancers working independently.
- Dancers in established dance companies.
- Teachers of education units of companies.

All the participants have been concerned with finding ways to gain knowledge and skills either to begin to teach or, for those already teaching, to improve their expertise to deal with the range and diversity of challenges with which they are presented.

After working with a number of dance companies, I thought it would be interesting to include some comments from those who lead the education work. I asked Darryl Jaffray, Head of Education [Ballet] at the Royal Opera House, and Dawn Holgate, Education Officer at Phoenix Dance Company the following questions:

- What do you consider to be the unique features of the education work of your department/company?
- What particular qualities do you require of your teachers?

First Darryl Jaffray.

What are the unique features of the Royal Opera House education work?

The Royal Opera House Education Department covers the work of both the Royal Ballet and the Royal Opera. The art forms are seen as complementary and although some individual members of staff have specialist art form knowledge, all staff work in close collaboration. Royal Opera House artists are used extensively within the education programme. Most dancers, singers and orchestral players, and many of the House's craftspeople and administrators are involved in talks, demonstrations, courses and creative projects. Education is a stated part of Royal Ballet dancers' contractual work.

Royal Ballet 'Chance to Dance' class. Photo: Deo Persaud.

There is strong emphasis on research and the development of the art forms, including the ongoing training of performing artists and creation of new music and dance.

The Department plans frequent collaborations across art forms and with other organisations. Examples include:

- Dance Bites Network 97, where young people worked together on composition, dance creation and design for public performance alongside the Royal Ballet at Bath Theatre Royal, the Wycombe Swan and the Lyceum Theatre, Sheffield.
- *Samsara* at Lewisham theatre, a collaboration between the Academy of Indian Dance, the Horniman Museum and the Royal Ballet.
- *Memories*, a collaboration with the Halifax Industrial Museum and the Royal Ballet, involving award-winning children's author Berlie Doherty.

Policy is devised and ways of working are continuously reviewed in the light of changing circumstances in dance and education in particular, and within society in general.

Individual projects are devised to address perceived needs, such as initial training opportunities in ballet for children who would not normally have access to ballet classes (the 'Chance to Dance' project). We try to sustain a balanced programme with individual strands as follows:

- Matinee performances with all tickets at reasonable prices.
- Activities aimed at teachers.
- Large-scale creative projects.
- Ongoing classes: Monday Moves (weekly classes for blind adults), Dance Clubs in Lambeth and Hammersmith and Fulham, 'Chance to Dance' classes from Mondays to Thursdays during term time.
- Introductory work (introduction to ballet demonstrations, workshops and study days).
- Publications, including packs, videos and CD-ROM.
- Courses, lecture series and talks.

What qualities do you require in your teachers?

I would divide this into those that are desirable but which can be taught and those that are essential and/or intrinsic.

Essential:

- Because not all dancers in the ballet world will have been taught in a thoughtful, learner-centred or creative way themselves, my first requirement is for someone who accepts and understands the need for this and is willing to continue improving their own practice.
- An in-depth knowledge of and respect for ballet and, even more importantly, an open-minded approach to what ballet *is*, what it may become in the future, and who it is *for*. A respect for, and knowledge of, other dance forms.
- I look for people who are passionate about the need for dance education work (they are not in it for the money!) and for those who like and respect other adults and children regardless of whether they are 'talented' or 'keen'.
- Humility! Participants should be the focus of attention and we do not encourage our teachers to behave as if they themselves are the 'star turn'.
- Teachers should be musical (not necessarily able to read music, although it helps) but I am happy to arrange further training and to seek help and support from our team of musicians.

Desirable:

- Given a choice I would prefer to employ teachers who are highly intelligent and articulate (we have a mission and need people to spread the word) but accept that intelligence takes many forms and that many people have been steered towards ballet because they are not academic ('she's not an intellectual but she has a wonderful physique, so should do well').
- Ideally, I would like people with highly developed skills in dance creation and analysis, but am willing to help teachers to develop these.
- If a teacher is to inspire, she or he needs to be an interesting and informed person. Wherever possible, we refer teachers to courses, performances and other activities that will enhance their knowledge, and we support them financially.

Now, Dawn Holgate at Phoenix Dance Company.

What are the unique features of Phoenix Dance Company's education work?

Workshop with
Phoenix Dance
Company at Potter
Newton Primary
School, Leeds.
Photo: Saluka Saul.

The unique qualities of Phoenix Dance Company's education work are embedded within the characteristics of its members. The majority of the company's dancers (past and present) are first-generation Afro-Caribbean descent. Many were educated at Harehills Middle School, where dance was a compulsory part of the curriculum for every child. The company is very much affected by its history and continually strives to maintain a balance between developing its future and acknowledging its past. Phoenix is the only repertory dance company in Northern England, and its work is renowned for its accessibility to a diverse audience. The dancers deliver the company's education work, which is intrinsically linked to the repertory. They recognise the importance of 'giving something back' to the community which invested in and supported them, and believe that the company's education practices should be not only accessible, but a challenging and fun learning experience.

What qualities do you require in your teachers?

Phoenix dancers have no formal teacher training experience. The dancers who deliver the company's education work have acquired their skills through observation and trial and error. Therefore, the type of qualities expected from a Phoenix dancer/teacher are:

- To guide, support and nurture their students through a positive learning experience
- The ability to articulate and communicate their ideas in a classroom environment
- To have some level of commitment to the delivery of the company's education initiatives
- To have a good level of belief and regard for the education policy.

A Training Programme

What follows is a proposed training programme that addresses some of the major areas of concern that I have encountered. Although the sequence may be seen as appropriate and logical, the order may be changed to suit individual circumstances. Attention must also be given to such questions as:

- What outcomes would be expected from such a training programme?
- How would it be evaluated?

The Programme

Each section of the programme is comprised of two related elements:

- Preparing for a workshop or course.
  Needs analysis.
- Structure of a creative/ improvisational workshop.
  Movement analysis.
- Technical training.
  Safe body management.
- Working with a range of groups and a variety of expectations.
  Progression and development.
- Composing short dances.
  Linking work to repertory.
- Engaging students in the activity.
  Responsibility and ownership.
- Evaluating a project.
  Enhancing practice.

In planning such a programme the amount of time and emphasis given to each element is likely to vary depending upon the background, knowledge and skills of the participants. It will also need to take account of individual needs, as well as those of the company or education unit.

The training programme should be spread over a period of time, so that the material can be assimilated and the opportunity made available so that the dancers can integrate it into their practice.

Bruce Joyce and Beverly Showers identify the levels of impact of training as:

- Awareness-raising.
- Conceptual underpinning.
- Acquisition of appropriate knowledge and skills.
- Feedback on performance.
- On-the-job-application.
  B. Joyce & B. Showers (1980), 'Improving In-Service Training', Educational Leadership, 1980.

Ludus Dance
Company summer
school. Photo:
Alan Dowthwaite.

It might be profitable to use this model as a guide when planning a programme. It will be necessary to determine the degree of competence achieved at each of these levels by the teachers concerned. For example, although much might have already been achieved at the first two levels, if work is to be undertaken in a new area – say in primary schools, or with people with special needs – some additional *knowledge and skills* supported by *conceptual underpinning* will be needed.

Experts in the field who could offer suitable training need to be identified. Some of this training might involve all the dancers or only be for one or two members of the education department.

Feedback on performance as teachers, can be undertaken in a number of ways, such as:

- Colleagues observing and commenting on each other's work.
- The client's responses.
- The participants' responses.
- Invited observer(s).

This may be done during training or at a workshop.

On-the-job application indicates ways in which dancers can continue to be supported in their working practice.

Evaluation

Such a programme will require evaluation (see Chapter 2). As indicated, evaluation is not just something that takes place at the end, but is integral to the whole enterprise. This will help to ensure that the learning involved continues, is not just a 'one-off'. Learning is a process, not an event.

Planning and Evaluating a Project

Good advance preparation given to planning a project can help to ensure its success.

Identifying the needs and expectations of all the participants is crucial. Considering if they have been met and the quality of outcomes is equally important. What follows is a planning form – intended for the person requesting the workshop – to aid preparation. This is followed by some examples of evaluation forms.

Planning Form

Workshop details
School/Centre/Organisation:
Address:
Telephone:
Contact name:
Position in institution:
Date of workshop:
Time of workshop:

What do you hope the participants will gain from this workshop?

Are there particular elements that you would wish to be included?

What will your involvement be?

About the Group

What is the dance experience of the group?

Give some indication of the nature and duration of any previous training.

How many will take part in the workshop? How many males/females? Is anyone excluded from participating?

Please indicate the age range.

Are there any with special needs?

Workshop facilities

Please provide a description of the workspace. Its size. The effectiveness of the heating? The type of floor.

Knowing Dance

Are the following available?
- piano
- cassette player
- CD player
- video playback

Please add any further information that you think would be useful.

Evaluation Form (Workshop Organiser)

Workshop title:
Date:
Your name:
School/Centre/Organisation:
Workshop teacher's name:

1. What was your overall impression of the workshop?

2. How satisfied were you with the quality of the visiting teacher's work? e.g. preparation, structure and management of class

3. How appropriate was the material, with reference to the age, experience, ability and interests of the group?

4. Were the students sufficiently interested and challenged?

5. What do you think that the students gained from the workshop?

6. To what extent have your expectations of the workshop been fulfilled?

7. Please add any further comments you wish to make. For example, how might the workshop have been improved? (Continue on the other side of this sheet, if necessary).

Evaluation Form (Student's version – Example 1)

Workshop title:
Date:
Your name:
School/Centre/Organisation:
Workshop teacher's name:

1. What did you enjoy most?

2. What did you enjoy least?

3. What did you learn from the workshop?

4, Can you think of ways in which it might have been improved?

5. Please add any further comments you wish to make. (Continue on the other side of this sheet, if necessary).

Evaluation Form (Student's Version – Example 2)

Workshop title:
Date:
Your name:
School/Centre/Organisation:
Workshop teacher's name:

1. On a scale of 1–10 (10 being the highest) how would you rate the workshop?

   1   2   3   4   5   6   7   8   9   10

2. On a scale of 1–5 (5 being the highest), give each part of the class a score.

warm up	1	2	3	4	5
improvisation	1	2	3	4	5
creating dances	1	2	3	4	5
performing dances	1	2	3	4	5
talking about the work	1	2	3	4	5

3. What would you have liked more of?

                    less of?

4. Please add any further comments you wish to make. (Continue on the other side of this sheet, if necessary).

Knowing Dance

Evaluation Form (Teacher's Version)

Workshop title:
Date(s):
School/Centre/Organisation:
Your name:

1. What was your overall impression of the workshop?

2. Preparation and content. How a) effective and b) relevant was the material?

3. Presentation. To what extent were you able to challenge and stimulate the students?

4. Response of the students. How did the students respond to the material? What did they achieve?

5. If you were given the opportunity, how would you follow up this work?

Teaching: Self-Analysis Form

1. Looking at your role as a teacher, to what extent do you regard what you do as:

	totally	mostly	sometimes	never
Training?				
Instruction?				
Developing specific skills?				
Exploration?				
Concerned with enquiry?				
Therapy?				
Entertainment?				
Promoting attitudes?				
Imparting values?				

2. When teaching, how often do you

	frequently	occasionally	never
Use students' names?			
Encourage individual students?			
Encourage the whole group?			
Give individual corrections?			
Draw attention to incorrect examples?			
Give general feedback?			
Use the knowledge, experience and interests of the students as part of the session?			
Change the direction of the class?			
Change the pace of the class?			

Look at your responses – are you happy with them? What are you going to do now? Discussion with a colleague could be helpful.

Enhancing Practice

Good teaching requires us to be curious. Teachers should be concerned with developing their knowledge and skills. We need to find ways to keep our work alive and fresh; not to become too comfortable with the familiar but to consider new material and new methods – not only to keep our students actively involved but so that we ourselves remain interested and challenged. We need to think of ourselves as learners on a journey that has no point of arrival but is a continuous exploration for learning.

Ways in which practice might be enhanced include:

Self-evaluation:

This can be done at a number of levels and stages. You can make judgments about your effectiveness:

- In working with individual students.
- In terms of how you taught a particular session.
- About the achievement for the whole course.

Some questions to help your focus:

- Do I create a safe, informal welcoming atmosphere in which each student is treated as an individual? Do I use his/her name?
- Are the aims and objectives clear and achievable? Has my planning and preparation taken full account of them?
- Do participants feel confident and at ease with each other? How do I know? What have I done to promote it?
- Do I use a range of teaching styles and strategies to enhance the learning experience?
- Do I give sufficient time and attention to individuals? Do I offer help in a constructive manner?
- Do I ensure that students leave with a sense of accomplishment and a desire to return and learn more?
- Do I demonstrate an enthusiasm for the subject; for teaching; and for my students?

- Do I enjoy what I do and do it well? If not, what can I do about it? Can I identify my strengths and weaknesses?

From John Daines, Carolyn Daines and Brian Graham (1992), 'Adult Learning, Adult Teaching', Department of Adult Education, University of Nottingham.

Evaluation by the Participants:

- What are their thoughts (both positive and negative)?
- Analyse what they have to say.
- Are their comments fair, reasonable?
- Is there a consensus of opinion?
- What have you learned from their evaluation?
- What do you need to do as a result?

Compare your self evaluation with your students' evaluation of the programme. You might have been too self-critical.

Share the Teaching Experience with Someone:

Ask a friend or colleague to observe and to give you some feedback. Often dance teachers do not have the chance to share what they do with other professionals. This opportunity can be fruitful and, by articulating what you do and why you do it, it can give your work affirmation and perhaps lead you to consider new directions.

- Take every opportunity you can to observe others teaching.
- Attend classes/courses that will be helpful to your professional development.
- Be open to seeing learning as a continuous process.

If we consider teaching and learning as a journey, where we have not yet arrived at our destination, the travelling is more important than the arrival.

Photo: Adam Eastland. Contemporary Dance Trust

"We shall not cease from exploration
And the end of all our exploring
Will be to arrive where we started
And know the place for the first time."
T.S. Eliot, 'Little Gidding'.

Printed in the United Kingdom
by Lightning Source UK Ltd.
113431UKS00001B/3-112